THE CAT IN THE CHRISTMAS TREE

Books by Callie Smith Grant

The Cat on My Lap
The Dog at My Feet
The Cat in the Window
The Dog Next Door
The Horse of My Heart
Second-Chance Dogs
The Horse of My Dreams
Second-Chance Cats
The Dog Who Came to Christmas

THE CAT IN THE CHRISTMAS TREE

AND OTHER TRUE STORIES OF FELINE JOY AND MERRY MISCHIEF

CALLIE SMITH GRANT, ED.

Revell

a division of Baker Publishing Group
Grand Rapids, Michigan

Published by Revell
a division of Baker Publishing Group
Grand Rapids, Michigan
www.revellbooks.com

Printed in the United States of America

Library of Congress Cataloging-in-Publication Data
Names: Grant, Callie Smith, editor.
Title: The cat in the Christmas tree : and other true stories of feline joy and merry
    mischief / Callie Smith Grant, Ed.
Description: Grand Rapids, MI : Revell, a division of Baker Publishing Group, [2022]
Identifiers: LCCN 2022003602 | ISBN 9780800742430 (casebound) | ISBN
    9780800737931 (paperback) | ISBN 9781493438761 (ebook)
Subjects: LCSH: Cats—Anecdotes. | Cat owners—Anecdotes. | Christmas. | Human-
    animal relationships.
Classification: LCC SF445.5 .C379 2022 | DDC 636.8—dc23/eng/20220314
LC record available at https://lccn.loc.gov/2022003602

Some names and details have been changed to protect the privacy of the individuals involved.

Baker Publishing Group publications use paper produced from sustainable forestry practices and post-consumer waste whenever possible.

To Aleta,
who was allergic to cats but loved to
hear everything about mine.
Rest in peace, sweet friend.

CONTENTS

Contents

Contents

A WORD TO THE READER

Years ago, my husband and I adopted a feral cat who had been hanging around our home. Once she decided she trusted us enough to walk into our house, she would not be leaving—she would become a 24/7 house cat. Her adjustment to indoor life was not immediate, but soon enough she seemed to accept this as a good move—less stress, plenty of food for the asking, and humans at her beck and call. In turn, she rather quickly became a well-behaved kitty, which we appreciated.

As we approached her first Christmas, however, I wondered how the cat might react to the Christmas tree. We brought in a tall Fraser fir and let it stand empty for a few days to see what she would do.

She did nothing. She simply enjoyed looking at it, even after it was decorated. She would perch on the couch and watch us putter around the tree. She'd occasionally lift her nose to the piney smell. That's all. She'd fended for herself long enough, and it seemed she liked everything about this new indoor life.

And a tree? Not that impressive. She'd been hiding under them outdoors for months.

Our new cat especially enjoyed watching the blinking lights once they were strung. At the Christmas season, one thing is certain—in this darkest time of the year, the world becomes brighter and more colorful. Gold and silver and glitter pop up in surprise spots. Soft lights glow in the night. Christmas trees shine.

Personalities also shine during this season, and it's the cat's personality that we spotlight most in these stories. They star in plots and dramas that go well beyond interacting with an indoor tree. Yes, sometimes the cat and the tree have a moment, but there's so much more. In this wide variety of stories, we meet kittens and cats—some even appearing in Christmas morning packaging!—whose personalities and bright presence take over and delight the Christmas experience, and life in general.

You'll read about Christmas miracles, both large and small. We see Christmas through the eyes of one of nature's finest creatures—cats—and how they view ribbons and dangling things and even manger scenes. We see those cats through the eyes of all kinds of humans—including those who are not fans of the feline but who become fans at Christmas. (And isn't that the charm of the cat, to win over the unwinnable?)

We meet cats who seem to believe that decorations at Christmas are placed in the house for them and them alone! We meet kittens who keep a household young at heart no matter what is going on in the world. Cats who help other animals of their tribe navigate the holiday time. Cats who earn their keep by bringing "gifts" of hunting trophies to their astonished humans. A wise child who reminds her mother that barns with livestock always have cats, so of course there would be cats at the birth of the Christ child in a stable. And so much more.

My mother used to spout the adage, "Curiosity killed the cat." But she never failed to add the lesser-known line, "Satisfaction brought it back." These stories show cats in all their curiosity *and* in their satisfaction when it comes to the holidays.

It is my hope that meeting the cats and their humans in these stories will pull you straight into seasonal joy. As contributor Lisa Begin-Kruysman reminds us, "Life's most precious gifts don't always lie piled under a holiday tree waiting to be unwrapped. Some gifts wrap themselves around our hearts and remain there for a lifetime."

Indeed. Here is a book full of those kinds of gifts at Christmas. And most of them come in the form of cats.

1

The Cat in the Christmas Tree

Maggie Marton

The teenaged Girl Scouts fluttered around eight-month-old Violet. Bundled in her puffy rainbow coat and purple knit cap, our baby girl looked cherubic with cheeks flushed pink from the snowy weather.

My husband, John, carried her up and down the rows of trees arrayed in the Lions Club parking lot. Every year, we selected our Christmas tree from the Girl Scouts' fundraiser. And each year he wanted a smaller and smaller tree, while I wanted a bigger and bigger one.

This year, the first Christmas with Violet, I dreamed of an enormous tree tucked into our living room. I imagined Violet sitting under the tree, gazing in awe at the twinkling lights and ornaments dripping from every bough.

As John tried to steer us to the discount trees, the skinny ones with missing branches and bent spines, I found "the one" in the nine-foot-tall section: a full, fragrant Douglas fir. It looked like the kind of Christmas tree painted on holiday cards.

"It's perfect."

"It's big."

"It'll fit!"

We pushed the tree as far as it would go into the hatchback of our Buick SUV. The top spanned the armrest between our seats and rested on the dashboard. One of the Girl Scouts' dads brought us twine to tie back the branches poking Violet in her car seat. We drove home with the scent of evergreen filling the car. My dreams of a magical first Christmas for Violet grew as pine needles swirled around us.

"We're going to be vacuuming these up until next summer," John grumbled.

As Violet and I watched him yank the tree from the back, I'll admit, it did look a smidge full. The needles were shedding all over his car. But it was beautiful, and I could envision it decorated and twinkling in our living room. John, meanwhile, worried about fitting it through the front door. He worried about keeping Violet from pulling down ornaments.

Most especially, he worried about our kitten, Ripley.

Our older cat, Newt, never cared about Christmas trees. The first Christmas we had her, we assumed she'd futz with a tree, so we skipped it entirely and simply draped ornaments on ribbons around our kitchen. Once we realized she had no interest in the ornaments, we picked up a small tree for the table.

She certainly wasn't a saint, but Newt rarely participated in typical cat shenanigans. Too dignified to bat ornaments or chew through strands of lights, she chose instead to snitch holiday cookies and sip water from the tree stand.

Ripley, though, embodied the clichéd curious cat.

She joined our family a few months before Christmas. A friend posted online that a pregnant cat appeared one night in her barn. No one nearby recognized the cat, and no one claimed her. So, my friend gave her a safe space to deliver her kittens, then found homes for the mama and all the kittens—except one.

I showed the remaining kitten's picture to John. The left side of her face was dark, almost black, with caramel swirls. The right side was light with dark speckles. Her toes alternated black and white like piano keys. She was only a few months younger than Violet, so it felt like the perfect time and the perfect match. The two of them would grow up together.

"On a scale of one to ten, how much do you not want another cat?" I asked him as he looked at the picture.

We drove out to the farm a few weeks later to pick up the eight-week-old kitten. John chose her name, Ripley, to match Newt's name, the two main characters of the *Aliens* movie.

As soon as Ripley came home, she explored every inch of the house. She found nooks and crannies even Newt didn't know existed. Sometimes it took us hours to find her. She got herself trapped in boxes and closets and bins and reacted with a hiss and puffy tail at unexpected sounds. She shredded anything she could get her paws on. She bonded with our dog, Cooper, and treated Newt as her mentor. She wanted nothing to do with Violet; all the uncoordinated movements and loud noises frightened her.

That first Christmas, we knew Ripley would be the wild card. Her mischievous nature and insatiable curiosity posed a challenge, for sure, but I knew we could work around it.

So, that day we wrestled the enormous tree into our living room, paused to let John saw off a top section, and wedged it in front of our bookcase. The tree barely fit our tree stand. In fact, we couldn't use all three of the screws designed to hold it in place because it was a bit too thick in the middle. I could see the tension in John's jaw.

"In my defense," I said, "I never measure anything."

I knew we needed to give Ripley time to get used to the tree itself before we decorated. Sure enough, she spent the first day climbing the tree. She launched herself into it, clambered around the branches while it shook hard enough that I feared it would dislodge from the stand, and finally leapt out and landed on the top of the bookcase.

After a while, she lost interest. She poked her nose into the branches or scratched at the base every so often, but by the third day, she stopped climbing into the tree altogether. It was time to decorate!

We hauled the boxes up from the basement and tackled the entire Christmas overhaul while Violet napped. I wanted to surprise her with the magic of lights, ornaments, nutcrackers, Santas, the works. We unpacked and hung everything while she dozed. We transformed our house into a winter wonderland as quickly as we could.

When she awoke, her reaction was better than either John or I expected. She squealed. She pumped her dimpled hands. She kicked her feet. Pure joy burst out of her body. Not yet a walker, she wanted to be put down on the living room floor so she could crawl around and examine each thing at her own pace. She giggled the entire time. It was magical.

"Let's put her in her Christmas dress and try for a holiday picture," John suggested. We wanted to get a shot of Violet with Cooper and the cats under the tree. Over the years, with various animals coming in and out of our lives, we'd perfected getting a posed shot with an arsenal of squeeze cheese, strategically placed leashes, and hope.

I changed Violet and brought her downstairs. John stoked a fire in the fireplace. I corralled the cans of cheese and the leashes.

When I came back into the living room, there it was: the precise moment I'd imagined. Violet sat under the tree in her Christmas dress, the green plaid skirt arranged in a perfect circle, while she gazed up into the tree at the twinkling lights. Her chubby little arm lifted. She pointed at the tree and squealed with happiness. I started to feel tears well up. This was it. The first Christmas moment of my dreams.

Before my tears fell, Ripley skittered around the corner. She paused at the edge of the living room, momentarily transfixed by the glittering tree. As I reached for my phone to take a picture of the perfect moment, Ripley launched herself to perch atop the baby gate that separated the living room from the front door.

John turned away from tending the fireplace as I toggled to my camera app.

With the tiniest jingle from the bell on her collar, we heard Ripley launch herself from the top of the baby gate and into the Christmas tree. It wobbled. All the ornaments shook against each other. And then the tree tilted. Ripley, caught in a branch, thrashed to free herself. We couldn't get there in time. The entire tree, Ripley included, tipped forward and landed on top of Violet.

In the chaotic moments that followed, Ripley freed herself and skittered off—not to be seen again for hours and hours—and John threw the tree off Violet. She wailed as I looked her over, first for broken bones and then for cuts and scrapes. Cooper pranced frantically around the tree and us, while Newt snoozed away on the pillow nearest the fire.

We surveyed the mess. The toppled tree. The shattered ornaments. The screaming baby. The missing cat.

Violet settled. Entirely unharmed, not even a single scratch, she was our Christmas miracle. We plied her with snacks and nursery rhymes. I vacuumed up pine needles while John righted the tree. We cleaned up the broken ornaments and sorted them in piles to fix or toss.

That evening, after Violet went down for the night, we redecorated the tree. This time, we used only soft ornaments, those made of fabric or paper. The rest, the glass and crystal, the sentimental, would remain packed and stored for many more years.

Ripley, I thought, got the scare of a lifetime. After she emerged from her hiding spot much later that night, she never launched herself into the tree again.

Well, not that year, anyway.

2

An Unexpected Guest

Rhonda Dragomir

Mrs. Pitt frightened me. Blue hair and stooped shoulders did not diminish the authority she wielded with just a look or word. Meekly, I had followed her on an official tour of the parsonage as she shared both her wisdom and her expectations for the new young pastor's wife.

We stopped briefly at the kitchen sink. "See how this shines?" The elderly woman's sweet Southern accent would have soothed me in other circumstances. Her blue eyes gleamed only slightly less than the stainless steel. "I expect to see it look just like this the next time I come. And I'd better never see any bits of food in the trap." She smiled pleasantly, but I wasn't fooled. Terror took hold.

At that most inopportune moment, Kitty rounded the corner with a trill. Mrs. Pitt stiffened. "You know," she intoned, "no pastor has ever had an animal in the parsonage before." She wrinkled her nose and sniffled.

"Yes, I know." I shot her my most engaging smile. "I'm so grateful Kitty has been allowed that great privilege."

Kitty was sixteen, a beloved black cat my family rescued one frigid December when I was eight years old. I pleaded with my husband to request that Kitty be allowed to come with us to North Carolina, and pity for the new preacher's wife had miraculously swayed the parsonage committee to allow it.

Apparently, that decision was made over Mrs. Pitt's objections.

Kitty gave Mrs. Pitt's legs a friendly swish with his tail, and she recoiled. "I don't like cats," she said, stating the obvious. I gave Kitty a gentle shove toward his food dish in the pantry, and he was distracted enough to leave her alone. Our tour over, Mrs. Pitt paraded to her giant Oldsmobile and left. I didn't believe for a moment that Kitty was truly welcome in the parsonage.

"A cat is always on the wrong side of a closed door." Kitty proved the truth of Garrison Keillor's wry observation. Endless trips to the patio to let Kitty in or out made life tedious, and we surreptitiously replaced a window in the basement with a pet door. I didn't plan to let Mrs. Pitt see it. Pleased with his new freedom, Kitty explored the nearby woods like the predator he was. Though an "old man" in cat years, he was still spry and in good health. Occasionally I heard him head up the stairs with a particular meow. It meant he carried a "gift."

When a cat brings a kill to its owner, it's supposedly an offering of love. The appropriate response is to praise the cat for its hunting prowess. I'm afraid I most often greeted my cat with screeches and wild dancing during his presentation ritual. Kitty's mistress was unable to appreciate his generosity.

Our first Christmas in the parsonage heralded my debut as a hostess. The Women's Missionary Fellowship always had a party at the parsonage, charmingly dubbed a "carry-in dinner." I smiled at the name, unaccustomed as yet to different terminology in the South. I slipped in the substitute description "potluck" one day, and Mrs. Pitt glowered. I would forever be a hapless Yankee.

Mrs. Pitt's words during our tour rang in my ears as I scrubbed, dusted, and polished everything in sight—especially the sink—before the party. I wanted everything to look perfect. With only minutes to spare before the ladies arrived, I banished Kitty outdoors. I felt a twinge of guilt because it was cold but reasoned that he was used to being outside. He stood at the patio door, meowing and glaring at me, but I shut the blinds.

I shooed my husband out a few minutes later, since the party was "ladies only." He resisted, eyes aglow with thoughts of the delicious treats soon to arrive. I shoved him toward the door and shot him my most intimidating get-out-now look. With a peck on the cheek, he squeezed my hand and whispered, "Good luck."

I took a few deep, cleansing breaths before the doorbell rang with the arrival of the first guests. The fireplace crackled with warmth, cranberry-scented candles shone, and my Christmas tree was a glowing masterpiece. The ladies toured the entire house, as I knew they would, and I was confident they found every square inch sparkling clean.

Mrs. Pitt's arrival was the cue to begin, and she placed her trademark sweet potato pie on the buffet table with a flourish.

Following a brief prayer, the ladies filled their plates and gathered to enjoy the meal.

The parsonage had a large dining room, but there were so many women that quite a few had to sit in the living room, balancing their food and drinks on tray tables. Heeding the tradition of putting guests' comfort first, I took my place at the end of the line, loaded a modest amount of food on my plate, and joined them. Their gentle conversation and kind compliments about the beauty of our home helped me to relax, lulling me into a false sense of security.

In the last-minute rush, I had forgotten to latch the door to the basement. I didn't realize my mistake until a familiar yowl wafted up the stairs. I nearly knocked the contents of my tray to the floor as I flew across the room trying to beat Kitty to the door. I was too late.

Kitty dragged a mouse, still writhing, across my feet. When I shrieked, he broke into a run, and I missed when I lurched to grab his tail. He trotted into the living room, head held high, to show off his most recent catch. When he rounded the corner, pandemonium erupted.

Screams reverberated from the walls and women scrambled to climb up onto the furniture. Some women simply froze in fright, forks poised in midair as their brains tried to comprehend the sight. My first instinct was to call for my husband, but then I remembered he had been banished. I was on my own.

Ignoring my fear, I scrambled to capture Kitty, latching on to his furry belly with ferocity. He was so startled that he dropped the mouse, which then wobbled off toward the couch in a last-ditch effort to survive. One woman trampled both the couch cushions and her dear friend in her effort to escape the mouse attack. After a few steps, the mouse fell over, succumbing to its injuries. Perhaps it was just scared to death.

Eerie quiet descended upon the room as every eye turned to Mrs. Pitt. Her inscrutable expression did nothing to quell my anxiety. I wondered what it would be like to pack and be gone before New Year's Day.

The corners of Mrs. Pitt's mouth twitched. Instead of a glare, I saw a twinkle in her eye.

"Oh, y'all," she drawled, "just calm down. We said it was a carry-in dinner."

3

The Sound of Music . . . or Something

Lonnie Hull DuPont

Lucy was my Russian Blue cat. A few weeks before Christmas one year, this gorgeous, little blue-gray kitten simply showed up at our back door in rural Michigan, freezing and panicked. My husband brought her in, and we decided she was our Christmas present that year.

That may have been the best holiday season of my life, receiving this kitten and learning who she was. We introduced her to her new home, her new cat-sister, and Christmas. She delighted in all those wonders cats enjoy at such a time: the blinking lights, wadded-up wrapping paper, empty bins and boxes, and water in the base of the fragrant Christmas tree. She was the Christmas gift that kept on giving, as they say, because she turned out to be one of the sweetest pets I've ever had.

I began reading about Russian Blues. True to the breed, Lucy was gentle and beautiful. The books told me that she would be even-tempered, sensitive, and prone to bonding with one human in the house (I was that lucky human). All that was true. And Russian Blues dislike noise. Boy, did she. If my husband or I raised our voices, this usually quiet cat would run in from another room and complain audibly.

The Russian Blue has thick hair, described as double-coated. Like many cats, Lucy was a fastidious groomer, and all that hair caused a fuss in her system. So she was a cat who tossed up a hair ball from time to time, and she had a very specific meow that would precede the event—a long, miserable yowl. Soon I recognized what it meant when I heard it. I had enough time to get to her and catch her offerings in a napkin. Then I'd follow her and catch the second offering, since she always upchucked twice in a row. She was very cooperative about this.

One day, Lucy and I tested that meowing communication. In my young days, I was a singer. I gave it up long ago, until my husband and I joined a church with a choir. I started singing again in church. I sang as I drove my long work commute. I took voice lessons to strengthen my voice and to work on pitch and breath. I enjoyed singing again. Especially at Christmas.

On a December Saturday, as I did the dishes, I sang songs from our church's upcoming Christmas cantata and also from *Messiah*. These songs were not sung quietly, but it never occurred to me I would be too loud for Lucy. Until I heard it—a long yowl infused with misery. I first mistakenly figured Lucy was about to offer up a hair ball. I turned from the sink to find her sitting on the buffet. She met my eyes. "Are you okay, honey?" I asked.

Lucy turned her face away and averted her gaze. She wasn't going to vomit. Or maybe she was . . . but not because of her tummy.

Miss Thing did not like my singing.

I spoke to her. "Are you kidding me?"

She languidly turned her face back to me and gazed in my eyes for a moment as if to say, *I'm glad we don't have to talk about this anymore.* Then she hopped down and left the room.

I tried singing a few times more, only to get the same yowling reaction from my cat. I decided only to sing in the car and in church rather than offend my gentle cat's sensibilities. But I did keep singing.

Many years later our other cat passed away, and Lucy seemed bereft. She hid under the bed for several days, then became uncharacteristically clingy. She was aging at this point herself. We adopted two kittens to start a new generation of pets in our house, but we were also hopeful Lucy would engage in life again with creatures of her own species. It was a six-month adjustment once the kittens moved in, but eventually Lucy indicated that she liked having them around. She began running with them and playing again.

The little black kitten named Tiki fell in love with Lucy from the moment she saw her. Tiki's golden eyes went wide and unblinking every time her big sister was nearby, and she always tried to get next to Lucy, who at first hissed her away. But eventually Lucy put up with Tiki's constant, adoring presence and let her follow her and hang out next to her, as long as they didn't touch.

I enjoyed watching this relationship. I loved how Tiki would hunker down in the sphinx position side by side with Lucy in the same position. Every now and then, Tiki would turn those golden eyes up to gaze at Lucy—who ignored her but tolerated her. Once when Lucy came home from a couple days at the vet's, our other cat hissed at her alien scent and ran off. This isn't uncommon with cats after one returns from a hospital stay. But Tiki was not put off by the new smells at all. She followed Lucy everywhere and stayed right next to her, as if to say, *I think you smell wonderful.*

When the kittens were three years old, we lost our beautiful Lucy to illness. Watching Tiki become protective of her ailing big sister had been fascinating. Lucy would tuck herself into her carrier when she didn't feel well, and Tiki parked herself at the entrance like a furry guard—for hours at a time. When Lucy died, watching Tiki process the situation was again fascinating—and of course sad. But what was saddest for me was realizing I would never again watch those interactions between Tiki and Lucy.

I did notice, however, that Tiki seemed to have picked up a few things from Lucy. Cats do model for each other. Lucy was the only cat we'd had who ate grass grown for her in a pot. Tiki followed suit, though her littermate did not. When I brought in fresh grass, Tiki literally ran to it, just like Lucy did. Lucy liked to climb up the long body of my husband as he reclined, put her paw on his chin, and ask to be petted. After she was gone, Tiki did the same.

Then something happened that showed me another influence Lucy had had on her little protégé, Tiki.

I was back to singing in the house. One day I sat at the computer screen watching an old video of Shirley Bassey singing

"Goldfinger." My husband, Joe, joined me, and I began singing along.

"Goldfinger" cannot be sung softly. So I belted the notes out loud and strong . . . until, midsong, Tiki showed up. She stood on her hind legs, put her paws on my thigh, and squawked once. This was usually a quiet cat. Joe and I looked at her and laughed, and I kept singing.

Tiki jumped onto my lap and placed her paws on my chest, looked into my eyes, and squawked again. Whatever. I continued singing. Now Tiki pulled back and lightly sank her teeth into my upper arm. I was so surprised—she was not a biter. But then I realized she wasn't taking a bite. She was keeping her teeth in me and looking right into my eyes until I acknowledged her.

Or rather, stopped singing.

Once I quit trying to be Shirley Bassey, Tiki unleashed her toothy hold on me, gave a final squawk, and jumped down. Message received. Once again, I confined my singing to the car and church.

Until the pandemic, that is. I went on Zoom for church services in mid-2020. This meant I also started singing hymns at home—and although there was no Christmas cantata during the pandemic, there were plenty of Christmas carols. I tried to keep my singing volume down, but Tiki usually showed up anyway, demanding that I stop. First a look. Then a squawk. Then climbing up to look in my eyes. Then the sinking in of teeth.

Really, Tiki? Not even Christmas carols?

As I write this, Christmas is six weeks away. Last week I returned to church in person for the first time in almost two years. I had forgotten how pleasurable it was to sing in our grand, historic church with its high ceiling acoustics. A few days ago, the choir director contacted singers to participate in a Christmas cantata. There will be singers' masks and social distancing during practices.

I said yes. And I will once again thrill to singing as loudly as I want—away from the sensitive ears of Tiki the black cat, clearly trained by the late, great, beautiful Lucy.

4

Holiday Sparkles

Amy Shojai

Crash-galumph-galumph-skiiiiiiid-thump!

"Amy! Will you please get *your* cat before she tears up the house?"

I sighed and pushed away from the computer. My husband grew up catless. Mahmoud neither understood nor appreciated kitten antics, especially while he watched sports on the television.

Crash-galumph-galumph-skiiiiiiid-thump!

"Ameeeeeeee!"

By the sound of it, the eight-month-old delinquent had donned virtual racing stripes. She ran laps that traversed the carpeted living room and family room, slid across the oak floor entry, bumped down steps to the dining room, then finished with a claw-scrabbling turn around the slate-tiled kitchen.

Thumpa-thumpata-thumpa-THUMP!

Aha, a new path discovered . . . The sound grew louder as she raced toward me up the stairs and flew down the hallway to land tippy toed on the guest bed across the hall from my office. I peeked inside.

Seren(dipity) stared back with blue-jean-colored eyes. Then she self-inflated in mock terror and began trampoline calisthenics (*boing-boing-boing*) on the mattress.

I quickly shut the door, confining "the devil"—my husband's name for her—to my upstairs domain.

Back in June, a friend had discovered the dumped kitten napping in an empty flowerpot on the back porch and called me, her pet-writer buddy, for help. I had been petless for longer than I cared to admit. Email, phone, and fax lines kept me connected to my clients and colleagues, but I figured the kitten would brighten the long, sometimes lonely, workdays. Besides, as a pet writer, I needed a pet. So it was Amy to the rescue and love at first sight.

My husband wasn't so easily smitten. He still missed our elderly and sedate German shepherd but cherished the freedom of being petless. I convinced him a lap-snuggling kitten would be no trouble. Besides, the cream-colored carpet he'd chosen matched the color of Seren's fur. It had to be a good omen.

I was wrong.

The Siamese wannabe had no off switch. She talked nonstop and demanded the last word. She opened drawers and explored kitchen cabinets. She answered my office phone but never took messages. And she left legions of sparkle ball toys everywhere.

The colorful toys polka-dotted the stairs. You'd think a peacock threw up. The toys floated in the kitten's water bowl, swirled in the toilet, and bobbed in my coffee cup. And Seren hid sparkle balls everywhere to later stalk and paw-capture them from beneath household appliances.

Mahmoud quickly learned to check his shoes each morning before putting them on. He was not amused. I knew better than to suggest he should be grateful Seren stuffed his shoes with only sparkle balls and not—ahem—other items.

I'd managed to buffer the cat-shock-effect over the past months by keeping her in my office during the day and wearing her out with lots of games before Mahmoud came home from work. Weekends proved a challenge. By Monday morning, my husband reached his kitty threshold and welcomed a return to the cat-free zone at work.

But now the Christmas holidays loomed. Mahmoud looked forward to two weeks at home, two weeks of relaxation, two weeks of napping on the couch in front of the TV.

Two weeks sharing the house with "the devil."

It would indeed be a Christmas miracle if we survived with sense of humor intact.

In the past, we'd often visited my folks over the holidays, where we enjoyed a traditional snowy Indiana Christmas morning, stocking stuffers, decorated tree, lots of relatives, and a sumptuous turkey dinner. This year we planned a quiet celebration at home in Texas, so snow wasn't an option.

But I wanted to decorate with lots of holiday sparkles to make the season as festive as possible.

"A Christmas tree? Don't cats climb trees?" Mahmoud's you-must-be-insane expression spoke volumes. He'd already blamed Seren for dumping his coffee on the cream-colored carpet. Maybe matching fur color wasn't such a great omen after all.

But 'tis the season of peace on earth, and I wanted to keep the peace—and the cat. So I agreed. No tree.

Mahmoud didn't particularly care if we decorated at all since celebrating Christmas wasn't a part of his cultural or religious tradition. But he knew I treasured everything about the holidays. So we compromised.

Gold garland with red velvet poinsettias festooned the curving staircase, wrapping around and around the banisters and handrail. Gold beads draped the fireplace mantel, with greeting cards propped above. A red cloth adorned the dining room table, while in the living room, the candelabra with twelve scented candles flickered brightly from inside the fireplace. Other candles in festive holders decorated the several end tables, countertops, and the piano.

The centerpiece of Christmas décor was the large glass-top coffee table placed midway between the fireplace, the TV, and the leather sofa. The wooden table base carried puppy teeth marks, silent reminders of the dog Mahmoud and I still mourned. Since we had no tree, the table served to display brightly wrapped packages that fit underneath out of the way. And on top of the table, I placed Grandma's lovely three-piece china nativity of Mary, Joseph, and the Baby in the manger.

Grandma had died several years before, right after the holidays. Each family member was encouraged to request something of hers to keep as a special remembrance, and I treasured Grandma's nativity. The simple figurines not only represented the Holy Family but evoked the very essence of Grandma and every happy family holiday memory.

Of course, Seren created her own memories and put her paw into everything. It became her purpose in life to un-festoon the house. She "disappeared" three of the faux poinsettias, risked singed whiskers by sniffing candles, and stole bows off packages.

She decided the red tablecloth set off her feline beauty. She lounged in the middle of the table beneath the Tiffany-style shade that doubled as a heat lamp, shedding tiny hairs onto the fabric. As every cat lover eventually learns, fur is a condiment. But Mahmoud had not yet joined the cat-lover ranks and was not amused.

"Off! Get off the table. Amy, she'll break your glass lampshade."

Crash-galumph-galumph-skiiiiiid-thump!

Mahmoud had no sooner resettled onto the sofa to watch the TV when the whirling dervish hit again. The twinkling gold beads dangling from the mantel caught her predatory attention. Seren stalked them from below, quickly realized she couldn't leap that high, and settled for pouncing onto the top of the TV. From there, only a short hop separated her from the ferocious mantel quarry she'd targeted.

"Off! Get off the TV. Amy, will you come get *your* cat?"

Crash-galumph-galumph-skiiiiiid-thump!

I arrived in time to see her complete a second Mario Andretti lap. I swear she grinned at us as she skidded past. With the next drive-by, Seren stopped long enough to grab my ankle and execute a ten-second feline headstand while bunny-kicking my calves, then resumed her mad dash around the house.

Mahmoud glared. "I thought you said cats sleep sixteen hours a day."

I shrugged and hid a smile. Seren had already learned what buttons to push. Rattling the wooden window blinds worked extremely well, but now she needed only to eye the decorations to garner all the attention she craved.

Cute kitty. Smart kitty. Mahmoud wasn't amused, but I was.

She raced into the living room, leaped onto the glass-top table, and belly-flopped alongside my treasured Holy Family . . .

"Off! Get off." Mahmoud shooed the kitten out of the danger zone before I could react. This time, I was not amused.

Mahmoud knew what Grandma's nativity meant to me. "Decorating was your idea. Don't blame me if the devil breaks something," he warned.

Before he could suggest it, I caught the miscreant and gave her a time-out in the laundry room. We'd relegated Seren's potty, food bowls, and bed to this room and routinely confined her at night or when away. Otherwise, she set off motion detectors and the house alarm—or dismantled the house while we slept. Besides, Mahmoud complained that Seren's purring kept him awake at night.

I used a wooden yardstick to fish toys from beneath the washer/dryer to provide necessary feline entertainment during the incarceration. Several dozen sparkle balls—red, orange, yellow, green, blue, pink, purple—and the three missing faux poinsettias emerged, along with an assortment of dust bunnies and dryer lint.

I sighed. The kitten's age meant several more months of madcap activity, and I wasn't sure how much more Mahmoud could take. He only saw Seren at full throttle. He also suffered from "Saint Spot Syndrome," which meant he recalled only the happy memories of our beloved dog and overlooked potty accidents, chewed shoes, and other normal canine misbehaviors of the past.

Seren suffered mightily in the comparison.

I felt exhausted after the first week of running vacation interference between my husband and the kitten. Whenever possible, I kept Seren confined with me in my upstairs office, but that backfired. She would sleep in my office, but once downstairs she turned into a dynamo intent on pick-pick-picking at Mahmoud, especially when he ignored her.

The second week began, and as Christmas drew near, I had more and more errands that required my attention outside of the house. Mahmoud came with me for some, but other times he preferred TV.

"Just lock up the devil before you leave so she doesn't bother me," he said. "I don't want to watch her."

It made me nervous to leave them alone together in the house. I worried that Seren might commit some last-straw infraction, and I'd be unable to salvage any potential relationship. I loved her, heaven help me; she'd hooked her claws deep into my heart. And I loved Mahmoud. I wanted my two loves to at least put up with each other.

But as I prepared to leave, I couldn't find her. At less than five pounds, Seren could hide in the tiniest spaces. One time I found her inside the box springs of the guest bed. On that day—December 23—she disappeared and refused to come out of hiding.

I think she planned it. Maybe the spirit of the holidays inspired her. Whatever the motivation, when I returned home that rainy December evening, my unspoken holiday wish had been granted.

I found my husband napping on the sofa. On the glass-top table beside him, the Holy Family nested in a radiance of sparkle balls—an inspired feline gift of toys for a very special Child.

And atop Mahmoud's chest, quiet at last, rested a very happy kitten.

Mahmoud roused enough to open one eye. "Fafnir—I mean Seren—still purrs too loud," he grumbled.

Fafnir had been the name of our dog.

With a nod toward the overcast day, Mahmoud added, "At least *our* cat won't need to be walked in the rain."

Seren blinked blue-jean-colored eyes and purred louder.

5

The Convert

Andi Lehman

My father wasn't always a cat person. As a service-minded Navy pilot, he preferred dogs. He saw canines as protective, responsive, and smart—the only logical choice for a pet. But a homeless kitten from Ankara, Turkey, challenged his view.

We adopted Grungy just before Thanksgiving on my seventh birthday. Despite the derogatory name my dad gave him, the tiny cat I'd begged for cleaned up well. Grungy boasted long, multicolored fur and a sphinx-like face in which dark pupils widened and narrowed in two pools of green. He seldom meowed but instead spoke with his tail, twitching selected portions of it at various speeds depending on his mood.

That first Christmas, my father was not impressed.

Over the winter, Grungy earned Dad's interest by defending our urban block from stray dogs and feral felines. For his trouble, he suffered constant cuts and scratches, and he lost a triangular chunk from the tip of his right ear before he turned six months old. While Mom and I fretted over every wound, my father dubbed Grungy a "little scrapper" and introduced him to everyone as the guardian of our apartment building on Farabi Street.

Dad also noticed his prowess as a hunter. Grungy routinely caught mice and other rodents and left them for us on the windowsill or doorstep. He once killed a rat my mother spied lurking on the balcony during a thunderstorm. When she phoned my father in a panic over the sighting, Dad supplied an easy fix for the problem.

"Just let Grungy out," he said. "He'll take care of it."

And he did.

It was my mother who taught Grungy to come for dinner. At feeding time, she stood at the door and blew air through her teeth to make five staccato sounds—psss, wsss, wsss, wsss, wsss—like a child whispering a pretend secret to a friend. Grungy quickly associated the noise with food, and he appeared with lightning speed whenever he heard the sibilant summons.

Dad groused that Mom should have just whistled. Although he made the vocalizations with ease, he felt foolish as a six-foot, four-inch naval officer in full military uniform whispering to the world for no apparent reason. He took great pride in the cat who came when he was called, but he refused to do the calling.

Grungy never tried to force a close connection with my father. He didn't rub or swirl around our patriarch's legs as he did my mother's and mine. He greeted Dad at the end of the workday with a casual flick of his tail before trailing him into the kitchen, where my parents greeted each other with a kiss and set out hors d'oeuvres and snacks. Grungy watched them load a plate with cheeses and crackers and various relishes, but his real interest was the olives, both the black and the green. His tail swished and swayed along with the tiny fruits on the glass dish.

One evening, a green olive toppled off the counter onto the floor, and Grungy's patient vigil came to an end. He pounced on his quarry and batted it several feet toward my amused father, who rolled it back with his shoe. The olive wobbled, and Grungy attacked it—over and over—until he tired of the game and decided to eat his playmate.

Hunching over the battered oval, he tore off strips of the green flesh and chewed politely, saving the pimento in the middle for the final bite. When he finished, he ran a rough tongue across both sides of his upper lip and licked the fur on his feet. So began a tradition in our family that lasted for years. Whenever my father helped with the appetizers, he saved an olive for our gentleman cat.

Grungy cemented Dad's ultimate respect when the Navy moved us from Turkey to Providence, Rhode Island. After being lost in transit for almost a month, Grungy got a hero's welcome when he finally made it home in the waning fall.

But one of our neighbors appeared the next weekend with a dire warning. "I didn't know you have a cat," he said. "I must warn you to keep it inside at all times. My Saint Bernard is a cat killer."

By now, my father believed Grungy could handle just about anything, so he responded with a smile. "Don't you worry," he told the man. "Our cat can take care of himself."

It wasn't long before the premise was tested. At breakfast one cold December day, we heard a terrible commotion and shouting from across the street. Our neighbor's huge dog came bounding around the corner of their garage and spied Grungy ambling across our leaf-covered lawn. We stepped outside just in time to see the action.

The shaggy monolith froze in his tracks and fixed a wild eye on our cat. His owner ran out the front door, screaming, "Make it climb a tree! Get your cat up a tree!" Dad put his big hands on my shoulders to keep me out of the fray.

The beast barreled across the street toward Grungy, who turned and sat to face the attacker. Because his victim refused to flee, the massive hound had to slow his pace. Legs akimbo and slobber flying from his sagging jowls, he backpedaled to a halt just in front of our unflappable cat. The abrupt stop sent a spray of dried leaves whirling into the air above them.

For a moment, the two looked at each other. Then Grungy lifted a front paw, unsheathed his claws, and rapped the rude intruder right across his nose. Pulling his head back in surprise, the Bernard yelped. Grungy leaned forward like a prize boxer and applied another one-two swipe with both paws.

The dog wheeled around and fled back to his stunned owner, who grabbed him by the collar and disappeared into his house. The embarrassed man never said another word about his cat killer—or our capable cat.

My father feigned an indifferent attitude about the whole encounter, but Grungy received two olives that evening, dropped nonchalantly onto the floor when Dad thought no one was watching.

A few days later, when I entered our den on Christmas morning, I noticed a gift in the small red stocking I had hung next to mine under the fireplace mantel. Above the fuzzy white border protruded a package of catnip and a dangling tag that read "To Grungy, from Santa."

I looked at my father, already seated in his La-Z-Boy chair with a cup of coffee on the side table and his favorite feline on the carpet beside him. He leaned over to rub Grungy behind his torn ear. I couldn't see his face, but I heard what he said.

"I guess old Saint Nick knows a great cat when he sees one."

Years later, at the end of Grungy's long and interesting life, Dad's eyes glistened with tears as he laid the box bearing our beloved pet into the soft dirt of our backyard. An orphaned kitten from the Middle East did more than change my father's mind about cats. The little scrapper changed his heart.

6

The Chai Lai Christmas

Lauraine Snelling

"Are you serious?"

I stared at a teacher at Olympic College whom I had come to highly respect and appreciate, partly because of her love of students—and animals. Ah, the stories she had shared with us, especially those about the Siamese cats she bred. I had gone off to another college for my second year, but one June day she called and asked Wayne and me to stop by, as she had something to show us. Wayne and I were engaged and planning a late August wedding.

When we arrived, we were introduced to her dogs and her cats, the most beautiful seal point Siamese I had ever seen and friendly, something not typical of Siamese. As soon as I sat down, I had a cat on my lap blinking at me with stunning Siamese blue eyes. As my teacher was also Wayne's teacher and friend, she knew we were going to be dairy farming with a friend of mine. We chatted a bit, and she took us to see the latest kittens, whose eyes were just opening. I was down on my knees by the box immediately, talking to the momma and telling her what beautiful babies she had.

"Would you like one?" our teacher asked. "I would like to give you one for a wedding present. They will be old enough to leave their momma by then."

My brain went into overdrive. I looked up at Wayne, who shrugged and sort of nodded. I was far more of an animal lover than he. I stared at our friend, eyes wide, I'm sure. "I've always wanted a Siamese cat, but oh my word, are you serious?" I also knew what kind of money she received for her kittens, and that was not within our price range.

"I am serious. I would love you to have one of my kittens. What I was thinking was you could pick up your kitten after the wedding and before you move to your farm. I have two in this litter not spoken for, one male, one female. Take your pick."

I held each of them, but when the little female started to lick my finger, I lost my heart.

"Really, she'll be ours?"

"Really. I'll have her spayed before you come for her, and since she's not show and breeding quality, we won't worry about the registration papers."

"She sure is love quality."

"That she is. She is friendly, as are her dam and sire. You'll need to come up with a name for her and let me know so I can call her by that."

"Can we come see her again?"

"You most certainly can. She'll be wearing a pink collar from now on."

I named the cat Chai Lai because it sounded beautiful. I called our teacher to tell her the name I'd chosen.

Fast-forward through a summer that took "fast-forward" beyond my wildest imagination. When we moved into our first home, a twenty-eight-foot silver trailer on a dairy farm with Mount Rainier filling the horizon beyond our fields, our possessions included one young pig (not many couples get a feeder pig for a wedding present) and a growing Siamese kitten who was already trained with a harness and leash and liked riding in a car.

As we settled into our new life, Chai Lai enjoyed exploring the farm on the leash with me. While the cows frightened her at first, she got over that and sometimes rode on my shoulders. We strung a line between two trees and hooked her leash on that so she could be outside more.

Our cows were registered Ayrshires, and in the fall we took the best ones on the show circuit. We split the shows with our farming partners. At our first show, we left Chai Lai home with our partners and stayed at the show barns. On our daily call home, two days into the five-day show, the news was not good. Chai Lai would not eat for them.

So a Siamese kitten joined the string of cows, heifers, and a newborn calf at the shows. We tied her to the stanchion next to the calf, and a Siamese kitten with harness and leash drew more attention than the beautiful red-and-white Ayrshire cattle. When the waitresses at the restaurant where we ate learned of her, they sent bags of meat scraps back with us. "For that kitten of yours." She ate well.

As fall skipped into December, I realized I would not be going home for Christmas vacation like in the college years. For some strange reason that really struck me. We needed to create traditions of our own.

But where would we even put a tree and what would we decorate it with? As newlyweds, we found our money was more than tight. The lack of it was nearly strangling, as well as, in our case, the lack of space. I made some ornaments and hung them in the curved front window. Chai Lai batted them, a couple going across the living space. She sat on the counter and watched me bake. I'd never realized how expensive the ingredients for Norwegian cookies were—butter, sugar, eggs, almond flavoring, and cardamom. Yikes.

At least we didn't need to buy a Christmas tree. We went out in the woods and cut the top off a small fir tree, stuck it in a coffee can of sand, and set it on the narrow table at the end of the foldout sofa. Thanks to Chai Lai, we quickly learned that one two-pound can of sand can cover a lot of floor. So Wayne screwed hooks into the wall, and we wired the tree in place. Chai Lai perched on the shelf in front of the window and studied the tree.

A neighbor brought over half a dozen shiny, medium-sized round ornaments, which I hung on our little tree. We had no lights for it, but oh well. Within a day or two, we had no ornaments either. Chai Lai delighted at the shattering noise. I swept them up quickly to keep her from cutting her paws. The same neighbor brought over tinsel. Surely that would not break. But when I caught Chai Lai with a silver string hanging from her mouth, no more tinsel.

A friend and I used construction paper to make paper

chains, stars, and balls. I made a star and covered it with tinfoil for the top of the tree. Teeth marks gave it more glitter.

The busier I kept, the less time I had to think about not going home for Christmas. The church we attended, a good hour away, did not have a midnight service, a tradition since my childhood. With cows to milk and chores to do, we could not get there in time for a seven o'clock service. More traditions down the drain.

Chai Lai batted more ornaments, balls made of squished tinfoil, off the tree.

"Look here, cat," I said firmly. "That Christmas tree is not for your entertainment." She sat on the window shelf and blinked her Siamese blue eyes at me . . . and purred.

I fixed plates of my Norwegian sandbakkels, Scotch shortbread, and Russian tea cakes, along with almond-flavored Christmas tree cookies. My mother had sent me an early Christmas present—a cookie press that matched the one I used growing up. Wayne and I passed out the treats to our partners, a neighbor friend, and Granny, the elderly woman who tried to help decorate our tree. I baked Wayne an apple pie as his gift, and we settled in for Christmas Eve. Gifts that had come in the mail were stacked under the table that held the near-naked tree.

Chai Lai, who was now allowed outside by herself, announced her presence at the door. Wayne swung the door open, and our bright-eyed cat jumped up the steps, mouse in mouth. Tail straight in the air, she padded over to me and laid the mouse at my feet, then looked up at me. If cats could smile, hers went from ear to ear.

"At least it's dead," Wayne said, trying not to laugh.

I squatted down to pet our cat, who was now seated and cleaning her dark paws. When I reached for the mouse, she batted at my hand, claws sheathed. I looked up at Wayne, and he shrugged. "Big help you are." And we both broke out laughing.

We ate our dinner, then sat on the sofa to open presents. Chai Lai jumped up from the couch to the window shelf, her favorite place, watching over our shoulders. I scrunched up some wrapping paper and flipped it over my shoulder for her to bat around. The first box wore a tag that said "Open before Christmas."

Together we opened it to find an angel with gold tinfoil wings, her skirts of plastic straws sprinkled with gold glitter. Carefully we fitted our angel on the top of the tree. Another box had three ornaments—a tree, a ball, and a box, all sewn and stuffed. We hung those on other branches. Chai Lai watched to make sure we were doing it right.

The last present was hers. A dangle to hang for her to bat at. Wayne twisted in another cup hook at the opposite side of the window from the tree. After we enjoyed our apple pie, I opened my Bible to Luke and began the story. "In those days a decree went out from Caesar Augustus that all the world should be enrolled . . ."

With Chai Lai curled up in my lap purring, we finished the story. I laid my head on Wayne's shoulder. Our first Christmas as a family.

But would the tree still be decorated in the morning?

It was, but to this day there are two sets of cat teeth punctured in the angel's gold wings. A new tradition? Every year when we'd put the angel on the treetop, we told our children the story of the Chai Lai Christmas. And some years, we even had the gift of another dead mouse.

a Christmas cat haiku

goal of the housecat:
find a spot of winter sun
and then follow it

7

The Boys

Claudia Fanti Brooks

just met the most beautiful kittens," my friend said on the phone. "Two brothers. They need a home, and I thought of you."

It was true that I had been wanting a cat. Actually two. And preferably males. My friend knew these details, but she also knew I hadn't been ready.

"I'm at my vet's office right now," she continued, "and I told the tech about you. She said she'll wait until you see them before adopting them out to anyone else."

I learned the kittens had been left by a client who could not afford to keep them. They were around three months old and had been fully examined, neutered, and vaccinated.

My previous two male cats had died a few years ago. Ever since, I'd played around with the idea of getting new cats. But it seemed like a big emotional step at the time. Not long ago, I had lost my sister to a long battle with cancer. At the same time, my first cat died, and not long after, so did my other cat. Then just before Thanksgiving, my son Max passed away from an accidental overdose of pain medication at the age of twenty-four. Very soon after all that, my fiancé and I broke up. This happened over a time span of less than two years. It was all too much.

I was close to my sister, and I missed her. But I was having an especially hard time with losing my son. Max was a wonderful young man. And he loved cats. He had been feeding a feral colony near his house, spending all kinds of money on their food. My own cats had been crazy about Max, crawling all over him anytime he came home to visit.

After I lost Max, I came close to adopting two Russian Blue littermates. But I could not take the final step. I was in too much grief. Now time had passed, and a wonderful thing had happened in the middle of all that sorrow. I met a man named Dave, and we were in a good and growing relationship.

Once I was in this happy situation, my friend started mildly nagging me about getting cats again. She's the one who had found the Russian Blues earlier, and she understood when I had to back out. But now she thought I might be ready. Was I? I agreed to drive to the vet's and take a look at those kittens.

When I got there, I was led to an examining room and introduced to two handsome tuxedo brothers. Even as kittens, they were lean and leggy and long. Both were black and white with pink noses and grass-green eyes, and they looked so alike that at first I couldn't tell them apart. The vet tech let them roam around the examining room so I could see how relaxed and playful they were. I took out my phone and filmed one of them playing with running tap water while the other one gazed straight into the camera.

I said I'd go home and think about it for the rest of the day, and the tech agreed to that. It was probably clear to her before it was to me that I would be adopting the brothers. I stopped at the store on the way home and stocked up on anything cats would need. So much for thinking about things "for the rest of the day."

When I got home, I texted Dave. He lived in a neighboring state, ninety minutes away, so I sent him the video.

His response: "Mine."

His next response: "Your only problem will be that they'll like me better than you."

I laughed and called the vet. I adopted the boys two days before Easter.

They turned out to be the best cats. I named them Mr. Skittles and Fancy Pants. True enough, they adored Dave from the get-go. They learned to like riding in the car back and forth between our houses, curled up together in a black and white ball.

Skittles became a husky guy. He was a little reserved, hanging back and watching his brother do fun things. Fancy Pants was extremely curious. He looked like he had on white bib overalls. When I picked him up, he rolled right into a cuddle position in my arms. He could leap high buildings in a single bound. Skittles watched his brother, tried the same leap, then fell like a turkey out of a tree, landing on his feet with a thud.

I found they never ran for the doors to get out. But sometimes Fancy Pants disappeared in the house. Once he spent twelve hours in a T-shirt drawer. I guess he was comfortable. Another time, he spent forty hours in a bathroom vanity. When we finally found him, he still offered no fuss. Just waltzed out.

It was the next month after bringing the boys home that I received bad news. On my neck was a metastatic melanoma. I got the diagnosis the day after Memorial Day, and surgery was scheduled for July with an expected seven-month recovery.

During my recovery, the boys continued to be their entertaining selves, taking all the changes in stride. They played fetch and romped with one another, and they seemed to want me to watch them have their fun together. They were such a comfort that summer. Then ten days before Christmas, I was scheduled for a second surgery—an outpatient one in which my ovaries would be removed.

Knowing I'd be feeling pretty low after surgery, I decorated the house for Christmas beforehand. I love Christmas decorations. And the boys? Oh, they were thrilled. This was their first Christmas, and they were 100 percent positive this was all for them. They played with lights and skinny pink velvet ribbon with rhinestones. They rolled around on the white tree skirt—they loved the feel of that texture on their fur. They liked to play with spools of curling ribbon, but I monitored that closely for their safety.

Of course, being tuxedo cats, the boys were always dressed for success, so I did fun things for Christmas photos. They indulged me. They wore red and green bandannas for the camera. I took pictures of them wearing fur shawls around their necks, and they always cooperated long enough for the photo.

I returned from surgery to my beautifully decorated home with the best gift—the confirmation that everything was benign. During my ten-day recovery over Christmas and New

Year's, I had two nurses—my boy cats who looked like twins in tuxes.

Skittles and Fancy Pants still took things in stride, but now they showed other parts of themselves. It turned out that Skittles was a caregiver. Having a bad day? Skittles understood. Fancy Pants always loved lots of petting and still needed plenty of attention. But he also seemed to turn it around and give so much attention back to me. I am an anxious person by nature. But somehow, I was blessed with two completely laid-back cats.

On July 28, one year after the first surgery, Dave and I married on the shores of the Maumee River, a half mile from where we now live in Ohio. We've been happily married now for a couple of wonderful years. What a gift.

As I write this, we're coming up on another Christmas—the season when we celebrate the miracle of the Christ Child. Today I feel like I am living another miracle. Regarding my cancer, I'm now told that I am NED—which means there is "No Evidence of Disease." Another gift.

And on top of those gifts? The two best boy cats in the world.

8

A Christmas Princess

Patricia Avery Pursley

A week before Christmas with temperatures in the thirties, an email arrived from my neighbor Kari addressed to our neighborhood book club: "Does anyone know who owns the black and white cat roaming our neighborhood?"

Of course, being a rescuer of all animals of the world, I started hoping someone else would come forward to claim this cat so that I wouldn't be tempted. Kari couldn't keep the stray, who had invited itself into her garage for a meal and a warm place to sleep. A couple of days later, Kari reported that her vet gave the eight-pound, year-old female a good bill of health. Since the cat was about a year old, that gave her a December birthday. This was definitely a Christmas cat!

"She belonged to somebody," Kari wrote. Her spay scar was still pink. We speculated about how the cat came to be in our neighborhood. Was she a child's pet? We cringed at the thought that someone had just dropped her off, especially so close to Christmas. I remembered seeing this kitty a couple of days earlier. Her huge ostrich-plume tail made her appear to be one big cat. Eight pounds? Her weight must be all fur.

Just a year earlier, my husband, Tom, and I were devastated when we lost our sixteen-year-old tuxedo Manx, Isabella the Opinionated. She meowed in triplicate at TV politicians and napped on the cotton snow under our Christmas trees. And ironically, it was Christmas a few years before that when we lost our bobtailed SugarBear, who that morning cleaned her face then curled up on my lap for the last time.

I missed the quirkiness and joy that a cat's personality and semi-unconditional love brings—the hopeful looks at dinnertime, the soft taps on the shoulder for a 5:00 a.m. breakfast, and the soothing furry head rubs. Cat lovers know these traits and will gladly recite tales of their own storied cats.

But Tom had suggested we stay pet-free since we wanted to travel more. Actually, his exact words were "I don't want another cat." Part of me agreed so I wouldn't fret when we were away from home. But this stray was tugging at my heart.

I presented my case. "We could just give the kitty a foster home!"

He rolled his eyes. "Giving her a room in the proverbial inn would be in the spirit of Christmas, right?" He gave me a look and a little smirk.

I rang Kari with the news that we would foster the kitty while she tried to find her a home. Kari posted a lost-cat notice online and taped bright green "Lost Cat" signs at our street corners. I crossed my fingers that nobody would step forward.

A few days before Christmas, Kari arrived with a cat carrier and a litter box. "My vet said she doesn't have an ID chip, and she has to stay indoors because she's been declawed."

Where did this cat come from? Cats have their secrets, and I think they should come with a bio: "Dignified tuxedo cat, one year experience chasing catnip mice, hissing at dogs, and managing treat distribution. Hobbies: Olympic gymnastics and dispatching flannel snakes."

Kari unlatched the carrier door, and out stepped a beautiful longhaired creature with an air of royalty. The ostrich-plume tail waved a royal hello as she inspected our house. Her sea-glass-green eyes calmly checked the layout, and her long fur belied the tiny frame.

After the tour, she ate a bite of dinner, strolled under the Christmas tree to give the cotton snow a thorough kneading, then settled down for a long winter's nap. Later that night, she hopped onto the bed where Tom and I had settled in to read. She looked around as if something was missing, turned her nose up at the cat bed, and chose a bedroom chair for the night.

When I opened my iPad to read, the Isabella screen saver gave me an accusing stare. "You replaced me, didn't you?" Not even a blink.

No, no, no.

"And she's younger!"

She's just here until Kari finds her a home. And besides, it's Christmas.

Pouty stare. I opened my ebook and settled in to a Melanie Dobson novel before turning out the lights.

The following day we heard our visitor's minuscule *meow* for the first time . . . really more of a *me*, and her tiny purr was nearly undetectable. We would soon know just how apropos her *me* was.

Like a total stranger, she offered little eye contact and pulled away from touching. How could I have forgotten? Don't touch royalty unless they make the first move.

Each time the door lock clicked, she dashed for the door. On the second day she dashed and was out and down the block toward Kari's house before we could stop her. Great! I felt I had let Kari down. Using my best falsetto voice, I called "Kitty, kitty, kitty . . ." through the neighborhood, shook the treat bag, and alerted Kari.

It was Christmas Eve and getting dark. Colorful lights twinkled on down the block, and thirty-five degrees felt way too cold for a small cat. As I headed for home, my heart sank at the thought that she might be out all night.

Just before bedtime I checked outside once more. There she was, frantically pacing at our garage door. "Me, me, me!" Going straight for her food, she gave me a *Downton Abbey* look that said, *Thank you. Off you go now.* I was just relieved that she'd returned.

A few weeks later, after no response to the signs and postings, we decided to keep her.

Tom commented that there seemed to be something missing in this cat. It was as if she was a little wild and had spent much of her time outside with other animals and away from people.

We got a few more glimpses into her past. She napped on the bare floor, sat at a distance from her food dish as if expecting other animals, didn't recognize a catnip mouse, and jumped in fear at a toy flannel snake. We speculated whether she would ever truly warm to us. Despite all that, after weeks of pampering, we fell for her, and she . . . well, let's just say she started to accept us. HRH became "Princess," nicknamed Princey.

Six months later, Tom and I were taken by surprise when she turned a corner almost overnight. One day she declared my husband The King. She followed him from room to room, sat on his foot as he shaved, kneaded the carpet with a look of ecstasy while he dressed, and cried piteously at the window when he went outside. I, on the other hand, was the downstairs maid in charge of food and games for our little Princess.

After almost a year had passed, one morning Princey took up her usual post on Tom's foot. He said, "I can't believe I didn't want another cat. Every day we mention some cute thing she did." Of course, a King would say that. The Princess, who drags around a worn-out hotel slipper, would be insulted if she knew he sometimes called her Cousin It, the furry creature from *The Addams Family* series.

As for me, I have slowly earned more favor. She tails me into my office and uses my desk for takeoffs and landings to and from her luxury wall perch (that *I* bought for her). I'm allowed to pet her head, but I get the squinty eye if I try to pet her back or brush her. But at dinnertime, she sashays past me with sweet hopeful looks that melt my heart. What did I tell you? It's all about *me*!

Princey's sweet triangular face and big green eyes give her a quintessential innocent look. However, all that changes at bedtime when I bring out Snaky, the flannel snake-on-a-wand, now one of her favorite toys.

Her feline brain clicks to Jungle Mode when she hears "Snaky is looking for a cat." Trumpets sound, colors fly, and the

Innocent Princess transforms into Olympic Gymnast suited up as a cat. She dashes onto the mat, and her jaws of steel grab Snaky. She somersaults and with the snake secure in her teeth performs the difficult four-legged dismount, pinning Snaky to the floor with furry toes. A perfect 10! In the game of snake and cat, it's good to be the cat.

Recently, however, the Innocent Princess surprised us by cleverly stepping up her game and expanding the playing field to include our entire house. In the semidarkness, she speeds, tail high, down the hall, waiting in ambush behind waste-baskets, furniture, bed skirts, and doors, one eye peeking to scope out Snaky's advance. If I bypass her hiding spot, she might dash silently behind my back to her next ambush site. As the unsuspecting snake wiggles by, she swiftly launches drive-by swats, sometimes throwing in a run up the side of a chair before charging off. If she is really excited, she includes hilarious high-tailed, fur-flying sprints across the front hall with a commando glance to check my position.

Last year, she climbed halfway up our artificial Christmas tree before leaping off and taking an ornament with her. We'll see what happens this Christmas. My guess is she will be napping on the cotton snow before the New Year.

When bedtime games come to a close, the dust settles and the sweet Christmas Princess sprawls out to cool down. I catch my breath, prop up the pillows, and open my iPad to read. Once again, the Isabella screen saver confronts me.

Now I respond back: *I think you would like her. She is very opinionated, and she has your eyes.*

9

A Christmas Peace

Callie Smith Grant

Several years ago, my household adopted a pair of kittens. They were siblings and were very connected to each other. They kept close together most of the time, snuggling or buddy-grooming. I came to really enjoy watching them interact. I found watching them calming. Peaceful.

We named them according to their features. The silver tabby with the strong tiger stripes and a lemur-like tail we called Stryper, spelling it like a particular 1980s rock band. The black kitten, when gazing into my eyes, liked to raise the side of her upper lip and expose one tooth. We called her Fang.

I loved taking pictures of Stryper and Fang. One of the photos was accepted for publication by an online feature of a major national newspaper. In that image, the cats were curled around each other like yin and yang. It was a true expression of who they were as sisters.

If one cat was ailing, the other cat would initiate cuddling in what certainly looked like emotional support. Once I walked into my home library area to find them hunkered down, side by side, on top of a bookcase, literally cheek to cheek, looking at me. I was especially delighted to see that they'd chosen to sit on top of the shelves of books that were all cat-themed.

This togetherness went on for the first few years. Then Stryper somehow broke her front wrist. I don't know how a house cat breaks a wrist indoors, but it happened. She had to have her leg tightly wrapped for five weeks until one day she'd had enough and got her leg out of it herself. Fortunately, she had healed.

But during the injury days, the dynamic between the cats changed. Stryper had been more alpha, and Fang was always gentle and deferential. Now Fang was more assertive, and Stryper seemed nervous about it. They stopped touching each other. No more cuddles. No more buddy grooms. They might be on the bed or couch at the same time, but they often became territorial and competitive. This resulted in growls, hisses, and occasionally physical spats, which truly disturbed me.

When Stryper got her groove back, it got worse. She would run up behind Fang like a lion going after a zebra in those animal films on television. Fur would fly.

I didn't sign on for that. I wanted those sweet sisters back. I was very disappointed in this behavior, and it didn't change. I had to watch their body language and put something between them when their staring at one another got intense, thereby thwarting a potential battle. We often grabbed Stryper and gave her a time-out in the bathroom. It calmed her down. Until the next time.

When the cats turned seven, I had to accept that this was their behavior now. The buddy-grooming and affection were not going to come back. They were now middle-aged females who had turned into mean girls.

Soon after, a friend of mine retired and moved by herself to my small town in Michigan from southern California. She had some health problems, and it looked like this would be a good move for her in many ways. It also meant I had my old buddy back. In our thirties, we had been best friends living in an exciting city, but we had not seen much of each other in the past two decades.

For a few months after she moved here, we had the best time. She couldn't come to my house to meet the cats because she was using a walker and my house was not accessible. We planned for her to visit after she had physical therapy and would be walking better.

We planned for other things too. In our younger, single years, my friend and I had always celebrated Christmas Day at my apartment with a lot of other single friends. She was an amazing cook, and after dinner, we'd pack up leftovers and take them to the homeless people in the neighborhood. We enjoyed that so much and hoped to do something similar at Thanksgiving and Christmas here. We talked a lot about the upcoming holiday season. She was planning to join my church. She wanted to help with food distribution to the community there once she was stronger. So as we moved into November, we started talking about Thanksgiving.

But these plans were not to be. One day in early November, I went to my friend's house and found her sleeping. I could not wake her up. She was sent to the hospital in a deep sleep. I became the person helping with her medical decisions. I spent time with her in her constant sleep state. I got her apartment ready for her to come home. I even hung a Christmas wreath on the door. But she never woke up. She died the second week of December.

This bizarre turn of events was stunning. I felt numb. I began taking apart her apartment, and her relatives flew in to continue that. We took her pantry of food to my church for distribution. I knew she would have liked that. The final cleanup of the apartment was on Christmas Eve.

The rest of the world was in the throes of the holidays. Everything seemed to be moving along without me. When I would come home from handling things those weeks in November and December, I would sink into my recliner and turn on my heating pad. Usually a cat showed up and snuggled with me. But since they didn't like each other anymore, only one would be there.

Until the day my friend died, that is. I came home understandably sad and tired. Once I was in my recliner, feet up, Stryper hopped up and joined me. She settled down on my left thigh and armrest, facing outward.

Surprisingly, here came Fang. She hopped up on the recliner and gave Stryper a long look. Stryper only acknowledged with an ear turn. Fang hopped over Stryper to my right armrest. She hunkered down on my other thigh and faced me. The cats were almost touching, but not quite. And they definitely did not want to look at one another. I considered this peace in the valley a gift for the moment and was grateful.

It turned out that it wasn't a one-time-only. Any time I felt low and retreated to the recliner, one cat would show up, then the other. One cat would settle on my one side facing me, the other settled on my other side facing away. It was as if they were pretending the other cat wasn't there. Neither cat purred or gave me headbutts or kneaded their paws on me in affection, though they were fine with my petting them. They were simply stoic sentinels, flanking me at a time when I needed that very support.

I did nothing to prepare for the holiday that December except hang some lights. I did not sing in the choir. I did not send out Christmas cards. I bought hardly any gifts at all. I had all I could handle emotionally. But I did have peace in my home and in my heart when my cats joined me in my recliner.

I don't expect cats to think or act like humans. But I have observed cats enough to know that they are in sync with their human's emotions. My cats certainly were. And it seemed as if they had called a truce with each other when they attended to me, because they understood that I needed them. Many times, the three of us sat together quietly with strings of Christmas lights blinking around us. I so appreciated it.

That Christmas, in spite of everything, I had the sweetest peace in my house when my cats called a stop to their feuding. And happily, that peace was not temporary. Now, as we get close to another Christmas, they're still acting this way. If I have trouble sleeping and go to my recliner for a bit, here comes one, then the other, jostling and positioning themselves on me in a way that comforts me but keeps them from touching. They seem to know when I need this.

I didn't like it when my adorable cats stopped cuddling and communing with each other. It was a huge change in their behavior, and it took me by surprise. But now they've modified that behavior for my benefit. It's another change that I was not expecting. To me, it was a Christmas present. And I'll take it!

10

Possum

Nanette Thorsen-Snipes

One cold, wintry night, we found out just what I was made of. I can assure you, it wasn't pretty. My black-and-white regal cat, Possum, did the unthinkable—in my house.

But let me start at the beginning. One day in late summer, my then-teenaged daughter, Jamie, and her boyfriend brought home a little critter from a parking lot giveaway. At first glance, I thought it was a hairless creature. The black-and-white kitten had a long, stringy tail that looked more like a baby possum's than anything else. He looked as if his black hair was parted down the middle, and his eyes were as yellow as a harvest moon. They named him Possum.

Like all kittens, he was playful and got into things he shouldn't, but he was an indoor house cat and was never allowed outside—except for the time he escaped through the basement. We eventually found him days later, cowering behind our neighbors' trash can. Thankfully, he never brought any critters inside from our yard.

Possum was a curious cat, but he behaved relatively well, unlike our previous black cat, Nicky, who enjoyed bringing in any animal she could catch. Rather than kill it, she would be merciful and turn it loose in the house, much to my chagrin. I can't tell you the number of times she brought in live birds and allowed them to fly over my head, just out of my reach. I was terrified that one of them might latch onto my hair, so my husband, Jim, would chase them down and shoo them out the door for me. Nicky also brought in live chipmunks and set them loose in my office—and one time even a lone mole. For me, those critters looked too much like mice, and I'd call Jim home—more than once. Jim even left his nearby job to hunt down the mole, which we never found. I think that cat just liked to see me freak out. And I obliged her!

No, Possum behaved himself—well, most of the time. Once, while he was a kitten, Jamie and I took him in for shots. Afterward, he was so distraught that he pooped all over me, and I had to run to the vet's bathroom to clean up as best I could. We stuck our dirty cat into a cardboard box for the ride home. I reached down to reassure Possum that all was well, and he bit me. A cat bite mixed with poop called for a tetanus shot, which I got after I took Possum home.

Then came that cold winter night in mid-December, right before Christmas. My husband and fourteen-year-old, lanky son, Jonathan, decided to do some Christmas shopping for me at a mall about forty minutes away. I chose to stay home and enjoy some "me" time. I put on my nightgown and robe, fixed a cup of hot chocolate, and cuddled up with a book. The twinkling lights and Michael English singing "Mary, Did You Know?" lulled me into a peaceful place. I heard the rattling of Christmas paper while Possum played with the bright red and green ribbons. All of the Christmas sounds and sights made the words blur on the pages of my book.

An hour later, I dozed with the book slumped across my chest. All of a sudden, I heard a piercing noise. I sat up straight in my recliner, my heart pumping as if it were trying to hammer its way out.

At first, I couldn't discern where the sound was coming from. Warily, I rose from my chair and walked toward my son's room. I looked at his messy abode, full of clothes, a loose football and dirty baseballs, and his books. There in the middle of the mess stood Possum, with an innocence only a cat has when he's misbehaving. I stared into his large, yellow-moon eyes that, by now, were fixated on mine.

Upon looking closer at my innocent cat, I noticed a black cloth comfortably clenched between his sharp teeth. Aw, how thoughtful. My kitty brought me a Christmas gift—a black rag from my husband's workbench. As I reached down to remove it, the rag moved! And I screamed!

It was then Possum turned the critter loose, and a bat narrowly missed my head and flew to some unknown spot in my house.

With my heart pounding like a drum, I took off for the back door, grabbing my cell phone on the way out. Safely inside my car, in thirty-two-degree weather, in only my nightgown and robe, I gasped for breath and called my husband.

"Possum turned a bat loose in the house, Jim! Please come home!" I shivered from the frosty front car seat, praying he would make it soon.

His response was, "It's probably just a bird. We'll be home as soon as we're through shopping." His nonchalance was more than I could handle.

"No! You come home right now. There's a bat in the house." I put my hand on my chest, trying to remain calm.

"Oh, all right, we'll be there as soon as we can." I could hear the resignation in my husband's voice. He rarely took the initiative to go shopping, let alone with our son. Forty minutes later, I heard the car turn into the driveway.

He slammed his car door. "Okay," he said, "where is it?"

Jim was still confident it was nothing but a bird, but after scouring our small house for more than an hour, he gave up. I didn't. There was no way I could fall asleep knowing that thing might end up in my hair.

I searched through the bedrooms once again and then started looking in the kitchen. It was then I saw it hanging upside down near our kitchen cabinets. "Jim!" I called. "It's here!" My husband, with my son's help, cornered the creature with a broom and put it outside.

The following day, I realized Possum must have brought the bat up from our basement. He apparently didn't know what to do with it, except proudly bring his Christmas gift to me, his mom. What a thoughtful cat!

Possum and I had a long, hard discussion after that. And while Possum lived eighteen more years, he never once brought me another critter, at Christmas or any other time. For that, I thanked God.

a Christmas cat haiku
oh, the temptation
of dangling tree ornaments
what's a cat to do?

11

How I Rescued a Thief

Suzanne Baginskie

The last weekend before Christmas, my two children and I waited in line at the Santa booth in our crowded shopping mall. Christine had just turned nine and Alex was seven. Colorful holiday lights reflected in their eyes as they scanned the amazing North Pole display, and "Rudolph the Red-Nosed Reindeer" played through the mall's public address system.

Our yearly visit to Santa's Wonderland was a holiday tradition, but today my daughter had confessed this time would be her last. Nevertheless, I grinned as she took her turn on Santa's lap. When he asked what she wanted for Christmas, my daughter stared at me and said, "I really want a cat."

That wasn't at all what I expected. My husband and I were more dog people. Having a pet meant lots of responsibility, and I wondered if Christine was ready to take it on. I worked in a law office and didn't have extra time to care for an animal.

When I broached the subject on the drive home, Christine begged me for a cat of her own. All her friends had pets, she said. I told her I'd speak with her father and think about it. She sulked around the house for the next few days.

My husband and I decided to give in, without telling her.

On Christmas Eve, I hurried to the local animal shelter with last-minute hopes of adopting a new feline friend for my daughter. I shuffled past three rows of meowing, caged cats ranging from kittens to seniors. My lateness was on purpose. I needed to hide the animal for one night, so Christine would be completely surprised. I'd already purchased the necessary accessories like a litter box, food, and a comfy cat bed. A filled stocking hung on the fireplace and it contained a flea collar, catnip mouse, and more kitty toys.

When I arrived at the last aisle, a Siamese male about a year old leaned his front paws against the wired enclosure and released a piercing yowl. I stopped and admired him. He peered up at me with two pleading sapphire-blue eyes and a wounded expression. The attendant came over and released the lock so I could hold him. When the cage door swung open, the ivory-colored feline leaped into my arms.

He propped against my stomach, stood on his hind legs, and wrapped his front paws around my neck, simulating a hug. I stroked him. He purred and snuggled into my neck. Had he chosen me? I decided I'd look no further. As I signed the paperwork and paid his fees, the clerk told me he was recently rescued from inside a dumpster. How sad. I knew we would give him a good home and lots of love.

I'd brought along a green and gray pet carrier I'd purchased from a church thrift shop. I slipped him inside, and once I reached the car, I seat-belted him in the passenger seat. As I drove home, I thought about how excited my daughter would be to have her very own cat. I'd told her earlier that if I decided she could have a cat, she would bear the total responsibility for feeding, changing the litter box, and teaching the cat not to scratch our furniture. She promised me she would.

I arrived home, parked inside our garage, and phoned my husband. "Keep Christine busy so I can sneak in the cat." He chuckled. I crept up the stairs to our master bath, where the Siamese would remain hidden until the next day.

On Christmas morning, I tied a big red bow around the carrier and placed the cat under the decorated Scotch pine tree. When my daughter entered the living room and saw him, she paused and then squealed. "Hooray! You got me a cat!"

She hurried over to release him from his carrier, and the newly rescued cat hopped out and ran straight into her arms. He meowed loudly and licked her cheek. Buzzing purrs followed, and I knew it was love at first sight. Christine thanked us repeatedly.

She kept calling him Cat. I said, "You'll need to name him." She nodded. "I will, Mom. In a few days."

Cat adjusted quickly to his new home, or so I thought. About 2:00 a.m. the next morning, I awoke to a strange scraping sound, like a metal object being dragged across a tiled floor. I crept down the stairs to investigate and peeked into the kitchen. I flipped on the light switch to discover Cat, acting very brave and composed, holding my car keys in his mouth.

I'd set them on the hall table when I came home from work. He dropped the keys and, using his feline wiles, began a thunderous, pulsating purr before padding over to me. I swooped up the four-legged companion, scolded him, and returned to bed.

When Christine came down for breakfast, I told her about Cat stealing my keys and recommended she call him Bandit. She loved the name and agreed.

In the wee hours of the next evening, Bandit rummaging noisily throughout the house woke me again. I found him in the kitchen, pawing at something under the dining table. When I turned on the lights, my diamond wedding band sparkled at me on the floor. Lying beside it was my hair barrette. Since Bandit displayed such a high nighttime energy level, I decided he'd be better off prowling outdoors after dark. When we all turned in for bed later that day, I let him out to roam.

The following morning, I opened the door and cringed. The porch was scattered with objects all pinched by Bandit. He'd snatched a child's toy truck, a pair of flip-flops, and a screwdriver. None of the items were ours. I had my daughter pack the stolen goods in a box and place them in the garage. I wagged my finger in Bandit's direction and warned him not to steal anymore, but to no avail. The next week brought small Christmas lawn ornaments, newspapers, and a red plastic pail and shovel.

As the days wore on, we had to face the facts: Bandit was a thief, and his nightly hauls of loot were mounting up. I finally decided we'd keep him housebound at night.

Christine was upset, so we had a talk. I reminded her that the shelter had told me his history, that Bandit was abandoned by his previous owners. He was homeless and had to hunt for his food. By instinct, he was still hunting and rewarding us with his nightly treasures for adopting him. She understood.

Next I had Christine knock on the doors of our neighbors and inform them of her cat's scavenger ways. She suggested if something of value went missing, they should visit our house. Bandit gained quite a neighborhood reputation. When neighbors came calling, Bandit offered hugs to the same people he'd stolen from. Some of them presented him with cat treats, and they always departed with smiles on their faces and clutching their returned items.

We had all fallen in love with Bandit, and keeping him in at night solved everything. Despite his crooked ways, he kept giving my daughter those wonderful hugs, and she forgave his thievery. Because the first thing Bandit had stolen was Christine's heart.

12

The Y2K Christmas Cat

Deborah Camp

I t was that in-between time. Two weeks past Thanksgiving and well into the hustle bustle of the last Christmas shopping season of the twentieth century. Y2K madness gripped shoppers as they nervously stocked up on gasoline, batteries, and toilet paper alongside camping and survival gear. Would the new millennium bug really plunge everything into darkness after midnight on the last day of this year and reduce our technological society to ashes? That was the fear all over the world at the end of 1999.

But in my world, I anxiously headed home from Macy's, fighting traffic and beating back fast-falling snow that was overpowering my threadbare windshield wipers. I was more concerned about the weather than the predicted Y2K apocalypse. The weatherman predicted three to five inches of the white stuff, which was unusual and far too early in the season for the temperate mid-South.

As I pulled into the driveway, my thoughts turned immediately to our new feline houseguest. She had arrived on the front porch two nights ago—cold, hungry, bitter, and pregnant. The only thing missing was a cigarette dangling from her mouth to complete the look of haughty, immature indifference.

When my husband, Michael, scooped up the petite tortoiseshell cat and brought her inside, she didn't protest. After she was warmed up and fed a dish of wet food, he gently held up the small-framed feline and examined her closely. "She's pregnant," he declared, "and looks like she might deliver any day."

"Surely not," I protested. "She's just a baby herself." But when I placed my hand on her moving belly, I knew he was right.

"I guess Christmas is coming a little early this year," Michael said with a chuckle.

"I think Santa is playing a mean trick on us," I huffed. We had plenty on our plate already. Because we were small business owners, our work was *never* done—holidays or not. What if the Y2K bug really did knock out our computers, destroy our electrical infrastructure, and, as Michael joked, reduce us to burning our furniture for heat? Yes, finding suitable pet parents to take on newborn kittens in the midst of all this uncertainty was going to take a Christmas miracle indeed.

That evening we decided to name her Mali, but we often referred to her as our Y2K Christmas cat.

Mali's unexpected and queenly arrival threw our cat family of four—now five—into chaos. The male residents had no use for this small, intimidating intruder. I'd never dealt with a pregnant cat before and was impressed to see Michael clear out the bottom of our bedroom closet and set up a makeshift birthing center of old towels in a cardboard box. He left the door cracked open wide enough for her to slip into and inspect. The males circled warily, sniffing, hissing their disapproval, but Mali scornfully ignored them.

Apparently, the nest had met with her approval. As I removed my jacket and wool scarf that snowy afternoon, Michael emerged from the bedroom to announce four healthy kittens had been born while I was out shopping. Just like that, we jumped from four to nine cats.

We were soon dismayed to learn that new-mom Mali was neither warm nor maternal. Though young, she was street-hardened, suspicious of our motives to care for her and her babies, and contemptuous of the resident cats. The boys didn't exactly throw down the welcome mat either. It was now just a week until Christmas, but instead of baking and arranging holiday lunches with friends, I was watching over the four infants. Because of Mali's negligence, we couldn't be certain if she was feeding them regularly, which meant we needed to supply additional nutrients throughout the day.

Mercifully, Y2K was a bust. The end of the year came and went, and the new millennium was celebrated worldwide with nary a flicker in our little cat-filled world.

Despite the havoc brought on by Mali's brood, and the media's unrelenting Y2K predictions, we noticed throughout the holiday season a spirit of tranquility radiating from our oldest cat, Yellow Man. By the Eve of Epiphany, we discovered we could rely on him to help keep up with the kittens. Watching him stand guard, I was reminded of what Pope Francis once said: "God never gives someone a gift they are not capable of receiving. If he gives us the gift of Christmas, it is because we all have the ability to understand and receive it."

The moment Mali was done weaning her babies, she summarily dismissed them to pursue their own agendas, as she pursued hers. Yellow Man was still smitten by the tiny, playful creatures, and once they were released from Mali's dubious care, he became their substitute parent, lifelong protector, and best friend.

As Mali padded into her older years, her rough edges softened. Although she was never what you'd call a devoted mother, she remained a reliable constant in the lives of her twin calicoes, Flash and Spot. Her other two kittens had been adopted by a friend shortly after they reached eight weeks old—another Christmas miracle! Yellow Man remained the twins' favorite go-to family member, but it was always Mali who disciplined them. Afterward, she often issued long and affectionate grooming sessions as if to make up for her lack of attention in their younger years.

Today, our Y2K Christmas cat is a robust centenarian—the equivalent of a superhealthy senior citizen who eats right, gets ample rest, hydrates, and exercises regularly. She's outlived her offspring, all of the males who were there when she arrived, plus three other cats who became part of our family and have since passed away. Her frame is still small and trim, and as she glides throughout the house, she reminds me of the senior fitness walkers who ambulate the local mall. Her circuit winds behind ordained tables and chairs. She strolls a well-worn path leading to Michael's office and then upstairs to mine. Her walk rarely changes, and we can usually set our watches to match her promenade.

Our Y2K Christmas cat has aged with grace; she's less haughty and is more approachable. While at one time she didn't enjoy being petted or picked up, she now seeks attention and affection. In the late afternoon, the sun splays across the rug from the large window near my desk. Before finding just the right spot to stretch out and luxuriate in the sun's warmth, she'll first patrol my desk, daintily avoiding the keyboard, and position herself for a petting session. Though she doesn't always indulge, I usually offer some courtesy catnip.

I think back often to that Y2K Christmas and those weeks of kitty bedlam. Today most people old enough to remember can recount tales of families stocking up on canned goods, removing wads of cash from their banks, or buying backup generators.

But the Y2K millennium bug, which was feared to bring about the end of the world, instead kept us busy with a pregnant cat who paid no never-mind to the techno-panic hysteria. Her kittens distracted us from worrying about whether lights would extinguish coast to coast. And now, at age twenty-two, Mali reminds us of the many miracles we've experienced daily since she found our doorstep—love, hope, survival, averted disaster. And a new millennium.

13

Trouble for Christmas

Linda L. Kruschke

Just look at those giant ears. I think she's the one."

The note on the tiny black kitten's cage—"Warning: Bites"—failed to deter my son Benton. Which surprised me because bites from his first cat, Tom, sent him to the doctor for antibiotics. Twice.

As an added incentive, the adoption event was having a sale on black cats, so Benton's Christmas money from G'ma and G'pa would cover the adoption fee. The adoption team helper carried the kitten—dubbed Rosie by her rescuers—into the visiting room. She scrambled lickety-split to the top cube of the cat tree and peered out glowing-yellow eyes to Benton's steel-blue eyes. When Benton turned to say something to me, the kitten waltzed onto his shoulder and perched, as if to say, "Mine."

Benton refused to even meet any of the other kittens available at the adoption event. The warning sign, coupled with the wee one's history, left me skeptical.

It seems Rosie had survived a horrendous trauma. A band of street dogs attacked and killed her feral mother and all her littermates in a small eastern Oregon town. A young girl and her grandfather scooped her up and took her into their home before she could suffer the same fate. They tried to raise her, but they weren't cat people. They didn't realize you can't roughhouse with a kitten like you can a puppy and expect her not to bite whenever she felt like it. When she was three months old, they turned the kitten over to the local cat rescue organization.

"Let's maybe see some of the other kittens," I suggested.

"But she picked me, and she needs me," Benton insisted.

So our new kitten came home with us. Once there, she took one look at our cockapoo, Roman, and growled and hissed at him. The first night, we kept them separated with the kitten locked in Benton's room. It took a few days for them to negotiate a truce.

At the first visit to the vet we learned that Rosie was an inappropriate name for our new male kitten. After considering a number of options, Benton settled on Alucard, the name of one of his favorite anime characters. With his new name came a new attitude. Although Roman still thought he was top dog, Alucard now strutted around the house like he owned the place . . . and everything in it.

How many small items can one kitten steal from the top of a dresser? As many as you leave there. In the first month, I caught Alucard batting around a small decorative tile with a cross on it, which he'd carried from my bedroom to the kitchen floor. The next week, I discovered a small oval box open and empty on my bedroom floor. The pearl necklace that should have been in it was gone. I found it where he left it under the dining room table. I finally cleared the little things off my dresser and stored them safely in a drawer.

He didn't only carry things off to play with. He also knocked bigger things off my bookcase. Things I thought were safely at the back of the shelf and too high up for him to get to.

A Willow Tree angel became one of the worst casualties of his antics. Her name was Hope and she carried a lantern to bring light. The dangling lantern proved too tempting for a curious kitten.

I discovered the body first, lying on the floor in front of the bookcase. I scanned the room for her head and found it behind a chair. The lantern—Alucard's prize for his efforts—required a wider search. He'd carried it to Benton's room at the other end of the house. Thanks to a clean break and a little superglue, Benton restored Hope to her former angelic glory.

After that, I took to calling our cat Trouble, which rolled off the tongue better than Alucard anyway. When he chewed the spine of my small red-leather *New Testament with Psalms and Proverbs*, I'd had just about enough. Friends with cats assured me he would grow out of it, but I had my doubts.

If he was trouble indoors, he was double trouble when allowed outside. At five months old, we started letting Trouble—I mean Alucard—roam our backyard. His tendency to seek out the highest places in the house—like the tops of open doors or my antique wardrobe—perhaps should have caused us to be more cautious. He really did need close supervision.

One day Benton called me at work. "Alucard climbed a tree, and he won't come down."

Benton had left Alucard in the backyard thinking the fence would contain him, then had gone back inside to get a snack. When he returned to the deck, ham sandwich in hand, he heard a desperate meowing. He searched all around the yard but didn't see the kitten anywhere. Following the sound, he finally spotted Alucard thirty feet up a fir tree on the other side of our back fence.

By the time I got home, Alucard had climbed ten feet higher. It seemed unlikely his next move would bring him closer to the ground. I did what years of television taught me: I called the fire department. Surely, they would come, sirens blaring, and use their aerial ladder to rescue him. But it turns out that's only on TV. Instead, the dispatcher offered the phone number of a local arborist who rescued cats from trees as a sideline.

The cat rescuer came right away. For the minimal fee of $75, he climbed the tree using his state-of-the-art harness and rope system. I thought for sure Alucard would bolt even higher up the tree, but I was wrong. When the tree guy reached the branch where Alucard stood mewling nonstop, the kitten dashed right to him and gave nary a struggle as the man popped him into a sack.

Alucard undertook three more tree-climbing escapades that first summer. The last turned into an overnighter. He snuck out the back door right before we left to attend a wedding three hours away. We got home late. Benton thought he was in our room, and we thought he was in Benton's. We were all wrong.

We called the rescue guy—again—early Sunday morning. I suggested he should offer us a frequent customer discount. He disagreed.

We relegated Alucard to indoors only after that. Our mischievous kitten grew into a panther-like cat with a twelve-inch tail that he carried like a question mark. The question being, what trouble was he sauntering away from this time?

Alucard mellowed as he reached a year old. With the coming of cooler fall weather, he morphed into a lap cat. Much to my surprise, my lap became a favorite napping spot.

With the holidays around the corner, we talked about how to deal with our tree-climbing fool. I voted against putting up our artificial Christmas tree. I worried the dangling ornaments would tempt Alucard to resume his troublesome ways. I did not want to recreate one of the many internet videos of cats climbing to the top of a Christmas tree. Benton and my husband, Randy, outvoted me. As a compromise, I insisted no one hang any breakable ornaments on the lower branches.

I also had to figure out what to do with all my nativity sets. They weren't expensive, but some had great sentimental value, like the ceramic set my mother-in-law made the year my husband was born. I dreaded a king or shepherd suffering the same fate as my Willow Tree angel. To be safe, I placed breakable sets as far beyond his reach as I could put them. I set out an olive wood set from Israel on the low table behind the couch.

I was right, of course. The first night Alucard batted a wooden angel from a bottom branch. Then he lay down on the fluffy red tree skirt next to his prize and took a nap. I had to take a picture to capture the sheer adorableness.

Finding the olive wood baby Jesus on the floor the next day? Not so adorable. But at least it wasn't the ceramic one.

One evening in early December, I snuggled under a warm blanket in my recliner reading a book. Randy was working on thank-you notes for his postal customers who left him a Christmas gratuity.

I looked up from my book when I heard something clatter to the floor in the spare bedroom where we kept the printer. "Randy, you can't leave the door to that room open. The cat just knocked something over in there," I remarked.

He went to investigate. "There's no cat in here," he reported.

Hearing the commotion, Benton emerged from his bedroom. "What's going on?"

"Your dad left the spare room open, and your cat just knocked something over."

As he entered the living room, Benton laughed. "Mom, Alucard is on your lap."

Oh, so he was, fast asleep and causing no trouble at all. "Well, to be fair," I replied, "he's usually Trouble."

a Christmas cat haiku

tradition says that
on Christmas Eve at midnight
the barnyard beasts speak

14

The Nativity Cat

Andrea Doering

As a child, I loved all the decorations of Christmas, but I would spend hours in front of the ceramic nativity set made by my aunt. My imagination would settle on each figure in turn, bringing my version of the drama of the nativity to life each time.

This was a large set, with figurines eight to twelve inches tall. The soft glow of the iridescent paints used on veils and cloaks, the gold leaf on the wise men's gifts, the rough texture of the shepherd's clothes—all of it held my imagination and attention. Seeing the nativity set always showed me that Christmas in its true sense arrived. I knew it was Jesus's birthday, as our pastor would say, but when the nativity set came out, it was the Christ who arrived on the scene, just as he had all those years ago.

When I got married, I asked my aunt for a wedding gift no one else could provide—my own nativity set, just like the one I grew up with. It was a tremendous gift of love—the time and attention it took to make I likely will never fully appreciate. But every year when I bring it out, I am reminded of her talent and time. And as when I was younger, that sense of incarnation still happens. It's fair to say I revered this set, and perhaps too much! As our children were born and grew, I made sure to locate it where it would be seen but not touched. I didn't want anyone to mess with it and how it made me feel.

When Emily was about eight, she started making her own figurines out of clay. Just simple white modeling clay from the craft store—no firing in a kiln, and she didn't like to paint them. But even in that unfinished state, her talent was remark-able. Somehow, her little hands could capture proportions and gestures, and soon we had a growing menagerie on the kitchen windowsill.

That December, the nativity scene went up as usual, and my heart was happy. My eyes roamed on the figures, and I imagined again the story they tell.

I didn't look at it for a few days after that, busy with ordinary life. But when I did, I noticed there was a new addition. A small cat made of white modeling clay sat near the white cow, head cocked ever so slightly toward the manger, tail curled about its haunches. I knew who created it, but I wasn't happy with the predicament it created. This set, to me, was complete! And the scale of the cat was all wrong.

But how do you tell a child such a thing? I was pretty sure the baby in that manger would frown on crushing the spirit of a young girl. So when Emily appeared for breakfast that morning, I asked about the cat. "I didn't know you had made a cat," I mentioned. "It's very good!"

She nodded and smiled, the picture of confidence. "Those animals needed a cat. All the barns in my storybooks have cats. Now it's a good barn, a good place for Jesus to be born." Then she went back to her breakfast.

Emily's small, out-of-scale cat, unpainted and unfired, has stayed in our nativity setup. Turns out that the story I imagined as a young girl continues to capture the imagination, and it's never static. It is a never-ending story made new by every generation. What was complete to me was the beginning of the story for Emily, made better by a cat.

15

The Classified Cat

Lisa Begin-Kruysman

Long before the internet with its billions of websites like Craigslist, where many people now buy and sell all manner of items, people relied on print newspapers and their robust classified advertising sections. Listings for furniture, boats, homes, services, and even pets could be found among a host of promising columns. You could even find love among those old-school classified ads. A former boss of mine met her husband through a *PennySaver* ad. They even shared the same birth date!

Back in the late 1970s, my family found love too, when a gray tiger-striped cat named Morrison came to us through a classified ad in a local newspaper.

At that time, I was finishing the first semester of my freshman year at the University of Connecticut and had returned home for the holiday break. I was well aware that my then ten-year-old brother Matt had been given permission to get a kitten. A year earlier, we'd tragically lost our beloved family dog, Coco, and our petless home had a void that needed filling.

I grew up in Hackensack, New Jersey, in a house on Longview Avenue, named for the expansive view of the New York City skyline it offered. Although a mere thirty minutes from one of the world's largest cities, Hackensack offered some country-like qualities (one of my friends even had free-range chickens), and with my family's variety of beloved pets, our household was an unlikely Menagerie on the Hill.

Each of my three siblings and I specialized in specific species. I was the dog person with a fondness for rodents, rabbits, and birds. My sister adored horses. My brother John was our tropical fish guy with a large saltwater tank filled with exotic specimens, and the youngest, Matt, was our feline fancier.

I was excited about the prospect of spending a few weeks on holiday break getting to know our fluffy new kitten. Earlier that day, I'd been told that my brother would be picking up the new kitten that afternoon, responding to a "Free to Good Home" ad he'd seen in the newspaper. It was his early Christmas present.

I understood my brother's excitement. I recalled how I felt when I was Matt's age and eagerly looked forward to my own Christmas present of a tiny chocolate poodle we'd named Coco Puff. A kitten would be wonderful.

When I came home late that night, however, there in the multicolored blinking glow of the family Christmas tree sat a midsized cat. He stood and greeted me as if I were an old friend, rubbing up against my leg, purring like a motor.

Despite this lovely introduction, I felt let down. *This is no kitten!*

I learned the following day that my brother, upon arriving at the "Free to Good Home" location, had been a little disappointed as well. He'd gone there with the intent to leave with a kitten. But when he met this adult male, he'd been captivated by the young cat's majestic green-eyed beauty. So Matt brought the cat home and named him Morrison for the late Jim Morrison of The Doors fame. Living up to the reputation of that musical legend, Morrie quickly became a rock star in our world.

Christmas Day came a few days after his arrival. Morrie celebrated by swiping at sparkling strands of tinsel (remember that?) among the boughs of our big Christmas tree. He romped across piles of discarded green and red gift wrap, then wriggled on his back under the influence of too much holiday catnip. He did all of this with the familiarity that typically comes after a pet has spent years living under the same roof with their humans.

While our dog Coco had been high-strung and snippy, Morrie exuded a calm, take-it-all-in-stride approach to life. He was "The Fonz" of the feline universe. Many who claimed they didn't care for cats fell in love with Morrie.

"He's a cat that's more like a dog," a canine-loving friend proclaimed.

I agreed. Morrie truly was a "cat like a dog." He converted many a dog lover and taught me to see cats in a different light. Morrie was caring, sensitive, and sweet, always there to greet anyone who entered our home, making visitors feel special with his warm purrs and invitations to pet him. I recall times when I was upset or worked up about something, and Morrie would respond to my tone of voice, leaping up to offer comfort.

He was clownish. While I lay in bed reading the paper, Morrie would jump up and leisurely stretch his entire large body across the unfolded paper, blocking my vision as if to say, "Pay attention to me!" I'd always happily oblige.

He was confident. Like all our family cats had been, Morrie was an indoor-outdoor cat and street-smart. My brother John recalls a time when, while several blocks away at a friend's house, he noticed Morrie peering in at him from a basement window. Apparently, Morrie showed up there so frequently that this family, believing Morrie was a stray, considered adopting him. John of course informed them that Morrie belonged to *our* family. We figured that Morrie had on many occasions stalked my brother to this house and in doing so thought that if one of his humans spent so much time there, he'd consider it a second home too.

Over the course of several years, I always enjoyed my visits home in part because I looked forward to seeing Morrie. With each year, I observed the sleepy beast slowing down. He didn't demand to go out as often and preferred long naps in shafts of sunlight to hunting or guarding his turf.

On one late summer visit, I understood that Morrie, now well over twenty years of age, was saying goodbye to me. Half his former size and sluggish, he seemed to perk up when he saw me. Nearly blind, he followed me around the house and then outside to the garden with an unusual urgency, talking to me all the way. Outside, we sat quietly among the tiger lilies, serenaded by the hum of cicadas. I took the opportunity to thank him for all his years of friendship and to apologize for not giving him the welcome he'd deserved so many years earlier when he'd joined our family on that cold December night just before Christmas.

Not long after, my mother called to inform me that Morrie had slipped out one night and never returned. He came to us through a classified ad, lived life on his own terms, and chose to leave that way too.

He converted many a dog lover, including myself, leading me to appreciate the unique qualities of a good cat. He also instilled in me the knowledge that older animals make great companions. I learned to be open-minded when considering a new addition. We never know what gifts they may bear if we don't give them a chance.

Recently, I found a photo of my late brother Matt and Morrie. They are lying on the ground on a later Christmas morning, a boy and his cat afloat on a private island of joy, surrounded by discarded empty boxes and shreds of gift wrap.

Life's most precious gifts don't always lie piled under a holiday tree waiting to be unwrapped. Some gifts wrap themselves around our hearts and remain there for a lifetime.

16

Etcetera

Sherri Gallagher

want a kitten!" My ten-year-old big sister stood with hands on hips and a determined expression as she faced down our parents.

"Sweetie, a kitten will never survive with the dogs," Dad responded. "They're so big the kitten could get hurt. You can pet Sig or Mounty instead," he said, referring to two of our adult shepherds.

Dad was a German shepherd breeder, and we always had six adult dogs and scads of puppies. We lived way out in the country in upstate New York, and the dogs were loose most of the time. Back then, few people kept litter boxes or had house cats. Cats were let outside for most of the day and came back inside to control rodents at night.

"Janice has horses," Sister said. "They have a litter of kittens, and they don't have any problems. Horses are way bigger than dogs. I don't want to pet a stinky old dog. I want a kitten, and Janice said I can have one of hers for free." Sister had clearly gathered her facts and planned her side of the discussion.

Eventually our parents capitulated, and a small, white, fluffy kitten arrived. Sister was ecstatic making all sorts of plans for the delicate little ball of fur.

It was not to be. The kitten was let out, and the female dogs immediately assumed it was a lost puppy. They would pick the kitten up with its whole head in their mouths and put it in with the current litter of pups. After a couple of canine transports, the kitten headed for better climes, aka the neighbor's dairy barn. Mom and Dad talked with the farmer and found the kitten to be happily established and cared for. They decided it was best to leave the kitten in a better home.

Big Sister went back to work campaigning for another kitten. I think it was my parents who did the research and found a breeder, but as a four-year-old, I was oblivious to those kinds of things. However it happened, a Siamese kitten arrived on Christmas Eve.

Our parents wanted the kitten to be a surprise, so I was tasked with hiding the little creature until Christmas morning. The kitten was a sturdy little fellow for ten weeks old. When I took him into the kitchen, he proceeded to catch a mouse and drop it on my feet. I thought it was his idea of a Christmas present.

My parents awoke my sister Christmas morning by placing the kitten in her bed. She was delighted.

After some discussion, Sister came up with the name "Et-cetera" for her new pet, from one of our favorite movies of the time, *The King and I*, starring Yul Brynner. As the king of Siam, he would dictate letters and frequently use the line, "Etcetera, etcetera, etcetera."

Our bitter cold weather meant there was no way a young kitten would be able to survive outside for even a short period. So for that winter, Etcetera was a house cat. He was a wonderful mouser and grew at a steady rate. Etcetera was quite different from other cats we met. He would come when called and lie down on command. I would drape him around my neck like a fur muff or give him rides in my doll stroller. He took being both a hunter and a cuddler calmly and without complaint.

Late that winter another neighbor decided to burn down their abandoned dairy barn, which was infested with rats. Whether they burned the place down to get rid of the rats or to remove the barn from their taxes is not known. As a result of their action, big, aggressive rats invaded every house and barn for miles around.

Our house was under construction and had many entry points for the vile creatures. They were extremely aggressive. One night, sister walked from the living room into the kitchen, and a rat attacked her. She screamed. Dad grabbed up a machete he used to break up kindling and raced to her aid.

Etcetera went to work. He was still a kitten, but the rats were no challenge for him. He eliminated the rodents in our house. Then in the spring when he was let out, he did the same for the neighbor's dairy barn. He was so good at it that the dairy farmer came by and offered to buy Etcetera. A farmer buying a cat was unheard of—feral cats moved into barns and dealt with rodents. Of course, Etcetera wasn't for sale.

Etcetera eventually grew into a large cat. With his blue eyes and dark legs and tail, he was a beautiful animal. He was also quite capable of taking care of himself. When a dog got too close, Etcetera laid the canine's nose open. Once, a pack of wild dogs came up the road, and we had to call Etcetera back to the house since he was intent on stalking the creatures and explaining this was his territory.

One evening Sister was playing tag with our teenage cousin. As he closed in to make her "it," she jokingly yelled for our male German shepherd to attack. The dog, not understanding the concept of joking, started to join the chase. Dad quickly recalled the canine and put him in a down position. Etcetera saw the dog had been stopped, but apparently he thought Sister was still in danger. He launched himself at our cousin's face. It was a near catastrophe. When we finally calmed Etcetera, our cousin jokingly asked, "What next, the mice?"

It has been a long time since I've had a cat. If I ever do decide to get one, it will be a Siamese. And just maybe I will name it Etcetera.

17

Presents Galore

Kim Peterson

Ten years ago, we were helping our elderly cat, Biskit, through his last weeks and literally walking our dog, Cheyenne, in a padded sling through her final months. We had been through several years of job transitions, made a move from northern Indiana to East Tennessee, endured serious life-changing health obstacles and major surgery followed by a slow recovery, and now provided the heart-wrenching daily care for two frail pets. We had determined we were not going to acquire any more animals for at least two years so we could rest and recuperate. We needed to honor our commitment to Biskit and Cheyenne, then take a much-needed loooong breather.

So when my husband, Sean, pointed out two juvenile cats hiding in the thickets of our yard and under the neighbor's deck, I was concerned but didn't focus my attention on them. Our hands were full caring for two beloved animals who had given us unconditional love for almost nineteen years and fourteen years, respectively. Also, because one neighborhood resident hadn't spayed her cat or cared for the resulting litters, we had helped another neighbor in her effort to find homes for twenty-eight feral cats and kittens. I assumed these two were just more of the same, this batch born at Christmas.

We hit the sixties and low seventies many times that mild winter, so I wasn't troubled about these strays' welfare. They weren't going to freeze. But we became uncertain whether anyone was feeding them when we finally noticed that seeds and bread crumbs and torn-up pizza crusts placed in a porous bowl on a stump for the birds were being consumed by these two cats.

We immediately began placing kibble in the bowl several times a day. Once we went inside, a petite black cat led the way to the food, followed more cautiously by a small tuxedo who tried to make sure we couldn't see him. But with a brilliant white bib, four white feet, and a white snip on his nose, he wasn't as subtle as he hoped.

Winter melted into spring, and we continued to feed the two strays. Because no other felines had materialized, we came to believe they weren't born here but had been dumped in our subdivision by someone hoping they would find a home. Our animal shelter is now no-kill, but, sadly, it wasn't at that time. As odd as it sounds, dumping an unwanted animal gave it a better chance of survival.

We deeply missed Biskit, who passed in early March, but these two kitties added a bright spot to our final spring and summer with our dog. The steady access to regular food had produced a healthier coat on the little black female and a growth spurt for the tuxedo. Perhaps we lacked imagination, but we called them Midnight and Tuxedo, and they quickly figured out their names. Midnight came to the bowl to eat while we were there and had started allowing us to touch her. Tuxedo hung back but let us see him.

By summer's end, any time we were outside, Midnight would show up and watch us take care of our dog. Tuxedo, rapidly becoming a tall, handsome feline fellow, always lingered nearby. We believe that the foundation for their trust was laid during that time when we would relax outside with our animal companion. We sat in our Adirondack chairs beside Cheyenne, Midnight, and Tuxedo. Once the cats realized that this big yellow Labrador retriever wasn't going to chase them, they chased each other, tussled nearby, and finally flopped in the shade for a bath and some rest. Each day, they became more comfortable around us.

The months passed steadily, this routine creating sweet memories. As our southern summer heat yielded to more fall-like temps, we spent even more time outside, our dog often snoozing in the cool grass.

We worked on helping the cats feel comfortable near the house, which we felt would provide them more safety. We lived on the lower level of my parents' home, which meant our entry door with a slab porch and our kitchen window were under the deck facing the backyard. Encouraging the cats to hang out by us below the deck also provided them better protection from the weather. So, outside our kitchen window, Midnight and Tuxedo regularly met Sean when he returned from work each afternoon. "Treat time" deepened our bond. Sean petted the cats as they ate the tasty tidbits, helping them build more tolerance for human contact—and even enjoy it.

He always gave them their treats near or atop the Dogloo our dog had hardly ever used. During the interaction, he showed Midnight and Tuxedo how they could push through the flap and go inside. They didn't seem interested, but we lined the shelter with pillows and blankets for the cooler autumn evenings.

In early October, our beloved Cheyenne passed. We still sat outside because fall near the Smoky Mountains is gorgeous, and the cats expected us to be there. Sometimes, we just all sat in the yard together. Other times, a piece of tall grass turned into play time with us trailing it behind and one or the other feline chasing the seeded head.

With our dog gone, we switched our routine to placing bowls of kibble on the porch. We also served meals on paper plates there. Dabs of tuna or shredded chicken were greeted with a cacophony of purrs. A splash of milk, though first met with uncertainty, soon became an evening favorite.

We often left the door ajar during feeding times, hoping they might come inside. While they would occasionally peer in, no small paws crossed the threshold. But they eventually declared the Dogloo acceptable. Midnight and Tuxedo took turns regularly sitting on top, emerald green eyes peering into our kitchen window. As soon as we spotted one of them, we headed outside to play or provide food or both. They definitely depended on the regular meals, treat time, and interactions with us.

The beauty of fall faded into a much colder winter than when we met these kitties. As temperatures dropped, we often spotted Midnight and Tuxedo in a furry pile inside the Dogloo on cold days and nights. We smiled, knowing they were warm and safe.

We never thought of our time and money spent as gifts to these animals but as stewardship of God's creation. But all that we gave them must have seemed like amazing presents to these two cats who had struggled to survive: hunting rodents and eating insects; seeking shelter in the rain, storms, and cold weather; and seeking safety from dogs, wild animals, and people who are not always so kind.

All that year, we didn't realize they were giving us gifts too: trust, laughter, affection, and a soothing comfort for our deep grief. Gifts indeed.

What happened next surprised us. It began with a mouse the week of Christmas.

We're early risers, and one day, stepping onto the porch before sunrise, we discovered a dead but intact mouse. We wondered which cat had left it and if they would be back soon. With the cold temps preserving the body, we waited. But no one claimed the mouse, and we eventually cleaned it up.

On Christmas Eve, we received two more mice on the porch, clearly intended for us—one apiece. We joked about our early Christmas presents and, while we found it humorous, we hoped we wouldn't be receiving more holiday rodents.

But the mice arrived regularly the rest of December, throughout all of January, and into early February. Some were whole. Others must have seemed irresistible because they were mangled or partially eaten and harder to clean up.

These gifts were gruesome at times. But we gave the cats much praise. Then later, when Midnight and Tuxedo were elsewhere, we secreted the critters away. We didn't want them thinking we didn't appreciate their hard work and generosity.

An early spring arrived in February, ending the colder temps, and the almost daily gifts ceased. All told, we were given forty-four mice—some intact and some not—and one partial rat.

Presents galore!

Midnight stayed in our yard for two more years, then walked away one evening and never returned. Now an indoor and outdoor cat, Tuxedo remains with us, bringing an occasional "gift" to the porch in exchange for the good life he lives.

We can't eat pizza without Tux requesting some of the crust. Of course, we share and even add in some of the cheese and bacon. Milk, chicken broth, dry and wet food, safe sleeping. Tux daily enjoys his presents galore—especially the whipped cream!

Despite our plan to take a break from animals, two sweet cats came to us at a time of impending loss. They added humor and joy and love to our lives when we needed them. Midnight and Tuxedo, our presents from God.

18

First Christmas with Kittens

Debbie De Louise

They say having young children in a house at Christmas makes it special. I've found that's also true of having kittens in your home during the holidays.

Four years ago, a few months after my mother died, I adopted brother and sister cats, Harry and Hermione, from the Golden Paws Society Rescue on Long Island. They were three months old when we brought them home in October. Although we'd had other cats and currently had a male tabby, Stripey, whom we still have today, it had been more than twenty years since young kittens had lived with us. I'd forgotten the magic that kittens, like kids, could bring to the holidays.

To celebrate Harry and Hermione's first Christmas, I purchased a stocking with a photo holder and placed their picture inside. I filled it with a bunch of small cat toys and hung it on our stocking rack next to Stripey's, where our old Siamese Oliver's had hung the previous year before he left us from kidney disease. I felt sad replacing Oliver's stocking with the new one, but the kittens racing around the tree after one another made me smile.

When we emptied the stockings, my female kitten, Hermione, claimed a catnip mitten. She picked it up in her mouth like a mother cat holding her kitten and dragged it into a hiding place. For days afterwards, I found it in odd spots around the house and often caught her carrying it or tossing it up in the air and running to catch it. It's now raggedy and worn, and while other toys have attracted her, she still plays with and hides that Christmas mitten.

While Harry and Hermione liked the other toys in their stocking, especially the catnip snowman that Harry and our Stripey enjoyed, the boxes the family's gifts came in were an even bigger draw. As soon as one was opened, a kitten jumped inside. Hermione, the calico, who's always the first to try new things, was followed by her brother. I'd think the box was empty, but then a small white paw or black head would pop out as they played a kitten's version of a baby's peekaboo game with me.

Another attraction was the wrapping paper. Before I had a chance to clean up, the kittens romped and rolled through the paper, paws catching invisible prey as they ripped apart snowmen and reindeer, wreaths and holly.

Harry and Hermione had fun with some of the human gifts too. My teenage daughter, Holly, received a two-player tabletop soccer game that year that intrigued them. They gathered around it when it was removed from its box and batted their paws at the tiny men and small soccer balls, trying to remove them from the playing field. They also liked my daughter's new cozy blanket. It featured a pattern of black cats similar to Harry. The kittens took turns snuggling on it with Holly on the couch and kneading the soft cloth with their paws.

Besides the gifts and their packagings, Harry and Hermione were curious about some of the holiday activities in which our family participated. Baking Christmas cookies was a different experience with kittens in the house. Always open to new adventures, they watched with inquisitive green and gold eyes as Holly and I mixed the batter in a bowl and then spread it on the cookie sheet. We had to tap away small paws attempting to dip into the mixture.

Another thing the kittens wanted to get their paws on was our piano. It's not often used, but I like to play carols on it during the holiday season. That year, kittens walked across the keys. The sound wasn't too harmonious, but it was a fun prelude to our singing.

Holly wanted to dress up the kittens for the holidays as she once dressed up her American Girl doll. Hermione would have no part in wearing anything, not even a bow, but we managed to put a festive red tie on Harry. He looked adorable, and the red made a striking contrast against his dark fur. Holly snapped a shot of me holding our handsome boy in his holiday attire.

A tradition that the kittens put their own twist on was kissing under the mistletoe. We usually hang a plastic mistletoe over the front door, but that year I purchased a toy mistletoe stuffed with catnip and showed it to the kittens. They licked the mistletoe and then one another and, yes, they even gave each other kitty kisses. It was so sweet.

It didn't snow that Christmas, but we had a small storm earlier in December. The kittens jumped on the windowsill to gaze out at the white stuff on the ground. It was their first viewing of snow, and it was a cute sight to watch their wide eyes as they tapped the ice crystals on the panes, trying to touch them from inside.

When it was time for Christmas dinner, Harry and Hermione and Stripey were treated to special cat food and some cat treats. And by New Year's, what made the holiday season so special was that our ten-year-old Stripey finally accepted Harry and Hermione without growling or hissing at them. For the first two months that they'd been in our home, we'd gradually introduced them to the senior cat. Stripey had reacted defensively when they were together, but when they were separated, he'd play with Hermione's white paws under my daughter's closed door. The three finally made peace in December, a short time before Christmas, during the season that celebrates goodwill and harmony.

Today I look back and remember all the fun and activity that brightened our lives in that time after losing Oliver and my mother. I can honestly say that sharing the kittens' first Christmas was the best gift we received that year.

19

Kitty's Red Christmas T-Shirt

Karen Foster

A red, short-sleeved T-shirt lies in the bottom of my husband's dresser drawer. On the front of the T-shirt is a montage of sound bites from the movie *National Lampoon's Christmas Vacation*. I gave my husband the shirt as a gag gift because that's one of his favorite Christmas movies. He appreciated the sentiment, but unlike the movie, the shirt wasn't a huge hit. I think my husband wore it once.

But our cat? She adored that red Christmas T-shirt.

Or maybe it wasn't the shirt. Maybe Kitty loved our daughter, who once wore the large, baggy shirt to cover her pregnant belly. I only know the three were inseparable one Christmas season—Jenny, Kitty, and the red Christmas T-shirt.

Jenny and Kitty didn't begin on friendly terms. Our daughter had just left home to attend college when Kitty moved in with our family. Whenever Jenny came home to visit, our cat must have sized up this blond female as a stranger rather than family. Kitty abhorred strangers. Then again, she wasn't a huge fan of our family when she first arrived.

We'd always had felines in our home, but we'd never owned a feral cat until Kitty came along. My energetic nine-year-old son chose her, from all the other free kittens in the cardboard box, because she chased her tail while the others lounged. I should have known her feistiness meant this kitten wasn't going to snuggle in our son's lap while he played video games. But he wanted companionship. Someone to take the place of his two much older siblings who were away at college. How could I say no?

"What are you going to name her?" I asked him on the drive home.

The kitten had gray fur with a white underbelly, and her paws looked as though she was wearing white ankle socks. A white ring of fur marked her left side, reminding us of a store's trademark.

"Let's call her Target," he said.

We christened her Target, but we pronounced the name *Tarjay* with a French accent to add a little flair. Mostly, we would call her Kitty because she didn't answer to anyone but herself.

As soon as we arrived home, she ran behind our couch and refused to come out. My son thought he could outsmart her. He dragged pink yarn across the floor, hoping she'd chase it. His tactic worked until Kitty realized a grubby adolescent hand was attached to the other end of the yarn. She made a beeline back to safety.

Given a choice, Kitty preferred to live in our enclosed back patio so she could use the cat door whenever she wanted to go outside and roam the neighborhood. We had her fixed, hoping she'd settle down, but her free spirit would not be tamed. Over time—a long time—she learned to tolerate the hand that fed her. Mine.

Meanwhile, whenever Jenny came home, the two of them kept their distance. "Kitty has a split personality," Jenny said. "She's docile one moment and turns on you the next when you try to pet her. What a pill!"

Frankly, I thought the two of them were too much alike. They both enjoyed having their own space.

Years passed. Kitty's disposition mellowed with age, and she became a homebody. She also grew wiser. Kitty realized it was a lot warmer inside the house during the winter months. By then, the nine-year-old boy had grown up and left for college. The other two children lived far away. Kitty had plenty of personal space.

One Christmas season, Jenny, now married and six months pregnant, stayed with us while her husband attended a job training course. That's when Jen found the red Christmas T-shirt in her father's drawer and wore it daily around the house.

I've heard of a teacher's pet—a student in class whom the teacher likes best and is treated better than the other students. But I'd never heard of a Kitty's pet until that blustery December. Kitty could be purring on my lap, but if Jenny came into the room and sat on the couch, my finicky feline would move to my daughter's lap even though there wasn't much lap left to sit on.

In fact, Kitty became downright clingy. Or should I say—maternal? Even though she'd never experienced being a momma cat, Kitty must have sensed the hormonal change in Jenny's body and heard the baby's faint heartbeat. Because the way she sat on Jenny's round belly reminded me of a mother hen perched protectively on top of her nest. Other times, I'd find the two of them curled beside each other on the soft rug by the fireplace.

Christmas was around the corner, but our daughter had to leave with her husband and get settled into her new home before Baby Boy arrived. Jenny hugged her doting feline goodbye, but Kitty didn't understand. She roamed the house, searching for "her pet."

When I saw the red Christmas T-shirt lying on Jenny's bed, my brain lit up. I took a handmade scarecrow (about four feet tall, wearing denim overalls and a blue plaid shirt) out of the closet. I pulled the red T-shirt over the scarecrow's head and tucked his stuffed arms through the shirt's short sleeves. Instead of a straw hat, I placed a red wool cap on his bald linen head. Then I leaned him on the end of the couch where Jenny always sat. The scarecrow's dark eyes (drawn with a magic marker) stared straight ahead. His plaid-covered arms lay limp at his sides.

I didn't know if Kitty would care for him, but I figured he wasn't bad company.

"Here Kitty, Kitty," I called, hoping she'd leave her cozy retreat beneath our Christmas tree and voluntarily check out the dude slouching on the leather sofa. Kitty opened one eye and peered at me through the pine needles and silver tinsel. But she didn't move until I sat next to the scarecrow and patted my knee.

Kitty tiptoed over and around the wrapped Christmas gifts like she was maneuvering through a minefield. Jumping on my lap, her hairy body froze when she saw the lifeless person next to me. I didn't say a word. Kitty leaned toward the festive scarecrow and sniffed the air. She flicked her tail. Then she stepped on his denim legs and sniffed the red T-shirt that draped his upper body.

I hadn't washed the T-shirt, so I suspect the combined scents of Jenny and Kitty were woven in those red cotton fibers. Who knows what Kitty thought, but it must have brought back some affectionate memories. Or maybe that Christmas shirt felt like a safe place. Kitty curled into a ball on the scarecrow's sunken chest and purred.

I took a photo and texted it to Jenny. *Kitty misses you, but she likes your substitute. Must be the shirt!*

This scene wasn't a one-time photo op. Throughout the Christmas season, Kitty preferred lying on the scarecrow's chest instead of my lap. I tried not to take it personally. How could I be jealous of a scarecrow? Or a shirt?

Kitty exuded the picture of serenity when she lay there, purring with her eyes closed. If I'd put catnip or a live mouse into her tiny Christmas stocking that year, I doubt Kitty would have enjoyed them as much as she loved snuggling with that red shirt.

20

Miss P Saves Christmas

Anita Aurit

My sassy Siamese/tabby mix, Miss P, ruled the household and the hearts of everyone she met, including my mother. When I first held that tiny gray and white kitten in my hands, I declared her name to be Puddy Tat. She quickly made it known that neither Puddy nor Tat was an acceptable moniker for such a classy feline, and within a few weeks of her moving in, she was referred to as "Miss P."

When I lived in California, my mother, Miss P, and I often lunched together at Mom's house. Miss P was an adventure cat years before Instagram featured photos of hunky men hiking mountains with their felines in their backpacks. She was always up for excitement, and the sight of her hot pink halter and leash brought her running. She knew it meant a walk around the block or a ride in the car to Mom's house.

Miss P was the perfect luncheon guest, sitting silently in her designated dining room chair, gray and white striped tail wrapped around her front paws, the epitome of feline politeness. She'd slow-blink her eyes periodically to indicate approval of something in our conversation. She never demanded a treat; she simply sat, waiting for one of us to do the right thing, which was to offer something "feline approved" from our luncheon menu.

When lunch was over, Mom would sit on the sofa as Miss P settled into her lap. Mom would tell my cat how beautiful she was and how good she was while she stroked her in all the allowed places. My presence was irrelevant at such a time, and I always felt my role at these lunches was primarily as chauffeur. The vision of the stink eye I got from both of them when I had to say "It's time to go" is still with me.

Those lunches ended when Mom moved to Northern Idaho to be closer to my sister and her family. The distance didn't dilute the feline-human bond between those two. Every phone call included the question, "How's Miss P?" and a moment when I had to hold the phone out toward the cat so my mother could tell her how fabulous she was.

Eventually I prepared to move to North Idaho myself. I looked forward to spending a snowy Christmas in my new home with my sister, her family, and my mother nearby. Mom looked forward to seeing her feline buddy again.

I traveled to Idaho in October to prepare the new house. I drove up and spent some time with my mom. I was alarmed by her appearance; she was frail and had lost quite a bit of weight. My sister was worried about her and enlisted my help in attempting to get to the bottom of what was happening.

When I questioned my stubborn German mother about her health, she angrily responded that if there was anything wrong with her, she would tell me. She turned the conversation to Christmas and having all the family—and her favorite feline—together. She had crocheted little mice with catnip bags for Miss P and the other three cats in my family, Buster, Tucker, and Jasmine. She loved them all, but Miss P would always be her special cat.

I returned home and finished the preparations to turn the house over to the buyer. The accumulation of my life was packed in brown boxes stacked to the ceiling of the storage unit. This move was the realization of many dreams, and I was happy and excited. Life was good, the future was rosy, and Mom would be reunited with her favorite feline in a few days.

On the day my sister and her husband arrived to help drive the rental truck to Northern Idaho, I received a phone call. My mother was in the hospital. She was dying, and we might not make it in time to see her before she passed. We loaded the truck, packed the cats in the back of the SUV, and drove the 1,500-mile journey in record time, with only occasional stops. The cacophony of the four yowling felines in the back gave expression to the way we all felt. Every few hundred miles I'd receive a call: "She's probably not going to be able to hang on." Thankfully, the callers were wrong, and we had a couple of days to say our goodbyes to Mom.

The next few weeks were a blur of memorial arrangements, filling out paperwork, cleaning out Mom's house, and setting up my new home.

When the fog of grief lifted a bit, I realized Christmas was less than a week away. Miss P and I shared a love of Christmas. The moment I brought out the holiday trappings, she placed herself in a strategic spot to snoopervise the decorating. She observed her own special holiday traditions, swatting at the knitted kitty stockings, hiding under the ornament-laden tree, removing the candy canes from the branches, and chewing the ribbons on every present. The other three cats were ambivalent about Christmas. Their interests centered more on receiving their treats on time, having cozy places where they could snooze, and avoiding the vacuum monster. Christmas was just another day to them. Only Miss P and I truly celebrated the season.

After Mom died, Thanksgiving had come and gone with little acknowledgment. In a desperate attempt to bring some normalcy to my life, I dug through the boxes stacked floor to ceiling in the garage. We had put the Christmas boxes in the front so they were easy to access. As the snow fell outside and Christmas music played inside (all my Mom's favorites like "Silver Bells"), three curious felines surrounded me, waiting to hop into the emptied boxes. Miss P had no interest in boxes. She pranced back and forth, meowing in her Siamese voice, *It's about time! Get that stuff out and decorate my tree!*

As I hung stockings on the mantel and began to decorate the fresh spruce, breathing in the fragrant aroma of the Northwest, I went over the details of our annual Christmas contract with my feline diva. "I'm putting all the handmade wooden ornaments on the bottom branches for you. Swat and bat away to your heart's content. Leave the ornaments on the higher branches alone."

She slow-blinked at me, and I accepted this as her agreement to the terms.

"I'll put the tree skirt underneath. You might want to consider inviting the other cats to join you instead of hogging the space for yourself."

She looked at me, turned around, lifted her tail in the air, and marched away. Evidently sharing would not be part of the deal.

As soon as I finished the decorating, Miss P shot underneath the tree, claiming her spot on the red velvet fabric, settling herself in for the season.

After Miss P's tree was decorated, I took my morning coffee to the sofa, tucked my flannel-covered legs under me, and sipped the hot liquid, still tasting the bitterness of my grief. The same scene greeted me every day. A flash of silver and white fur launched itself under the tree. Two bright blue eyes winked from deep inside the spruce boughs, and a striped tail twitched and rattled the lower branches. A gray and white paw whacked an ornament, propelling it across the floor to land with the other displaced decorations. Miss P was enjoying Christmas, and she seemed to be saying that I should too. It took a while, but finally the day came when laughter replaced my morose musings, and slowly, very slowly, I began to engage in the world and the season again.

Miss P and I enjoyed seven more holidays together until she crossed the Rainbow Bridge at the age of nineteen. Today there are new felines in my life who "help" me decorate, but none share the same passion for Christmas as Miss P.

I cherish the memories of the amazing cat who didn't just save Christmas but saved me. Miss P, that sassy Applehead Siamese, restored my joy in Christmas and taught me that despite the losses and pain I experience in life, a purr, a head bonk, some feline antics, and the unconditional love of my cats are perfect antidotes for sorrow.

I still hang the "Cats Love Christmas Too" knitted stockings on the mantel every year, gifts from my mother many

Christmases ago. I sit with my coffee by my Christmas tree and imagine that there are visiting hours at the Rainbow Bridge. I close my eyes, picturing Miss P and my mother catching up while Mom's favorite cat peers through the boughs of a sparkling tree, taking the occasional swat at a decoration and sending it flying across the floor.

21

Panda, the Christmas Card Cat

Sherry Diane Kitts

I can't wait to see the Christmas card this year of Odin and his new cat.

My thoughts turned to my nine-year-old grandson with his chestnut eyes and ginger-auburn hair. Full of smiles and boyish fun, Odin brought joy to my heart every day. Every year I looked forward to receiving a Christmas card from Odin's parents complete with a yearly letter and a photograph of Odin.

That year Odin was getting a new pet. He'd saved his allowance so he could help his mom adopt a cat. I was anxious to see a picture of him posing with it by the Christmas tree.

I called my daughter, Amy. "When are you getting the cat? I hope it will be in time to get the cards ready for mailing."

"We're going to the animal shelter this weekend."

Amy had searched for a cat online, and she hoped Odin would be happy with her selection. I wondered, however, why she didn't want to get a kitten.

"Tell me again why you're considering an older cat. Kittens are fluffy and adorable." I imagined a little kitten jumping around and batting at dangling Christmas ornaments.

"Yes, they're cuties, all right. But with an older cat, I can see its personality and understand its background. I want a cat who's settled and not too frisky. One who can comfort Odin at night. Besides, some people don't want older cats. They're left behind. I called the shelter, and they said the one I'm considering has a sweet disposition. She's five years old and named Georgia. She'll be a great pet to adopt."

The shelter attendant informed Amy that Georgia had a home at one time, but for some reason had strayed or been abandoned by her family. The shelter found her a wonderful foster home. The foster lady didn't like the name Georgia and nicknamed the cat Panda. It matched her roly-poly black and white body. The cat had the same adorable charm as a panda bear. Panda interacted well with the foster family's dog, which was important because Amy also had a boxer mix named Maggie.

Odin went with his mom to the shelter, and they allowed him to sit with the cat. Panda snuggled next to him and rolled over to expose her tummy. She extended her legs and purred as Odin stroked her downy-soft fur. She didn't attempt to bite or scratch.

"This is a special needs cat," the attendant told Amy. "She has a small health problem, and her food is somewhat expensive. Will this be an issue for you?"

"No problem for us. What do you think, Odin? Should we take her home?"

He grinned and pulled the money out of his pocket. "Yes, and I like the name Panda."

The attendant turned her attention toward Odin and said, "I'm glad you're adopting her. She needs someone who will improve her life."

My husband and I arrived at Amy's the week of Christmas. As we placed our packages by the decorated tree, Panda came to greet us. She weaved in and out of our legs with her purr motor running on high. She welcomed our pats and nudged our fingers. She blinked in a genteel fashion and completed a few turnarounds like a model on a runway. We connected.

"Panda shows unusual affection," I said. "Most cats aren't this friendly. Did you isolate her to one area for a couple of days until she got accustomed to new surroundings?"

"No, she didn't show any fear," said my daughter. "When we got home, I sat the carrier down at the foot of the staircase, opened the door, and Panda walked out. She explored her new digs like inspecting a hotel room. She looked around each room, checked out the comfort of the beds, purred, and rubbed against my shins. I think she gave us a five-star review."

"Wow, I'm impressed. But what about Maggie?"

"They had a couple of bumps in the meet-and-greet, but now they behave."

"What happened?"

"As soon as Maggie approached Panda, her sweet demeanor changed. She hissed, gave a low meow growl, arched her back, and projected her cat hairs like porcupine quills."

"Oh dear. Did Maggie bark at her?"

"No, she just scooted backward. She wasn't interested in a feline challenge."

Maggie weighed seventy pounds and could have taken on a cat. But at twelve years of age, she accepted most things in stride. Panda had stated her case and declared her domain. To seal the deal, she pranced over to the dog's bowl in the kitchen and drank some water.

Amy said, "Maggie watched, turned, and eased out to another room towards her dog pillow as if to say, *Okay then, have it your way. It's time for my nap.*"

Panda accepted the invitation into the family without hesitation. She thrived with Odin's attention, and eventually even Maggie liked having her around. Amy knew they would give Panda good care, but no one knew the caregiving role Panda would assume.

Panda chose grooming as her favorite mothering characteristic. She performed different techniques to make any adjustments she deemed necessary for each family member. Whenever Amy applied lotion to her arms or legs, the smell signaled Panda to clean it off with her sandpaper tongue. Amy moved her away.

"Aghh, Panda. Stop it. I don't need washing."

Some animals can sense people's moods. After Amy put in a stressful day at work, Panda would make her way to her human's room and settle onto the pillow above her head. Other times she'd lay by Amy's side and stretch out her front paws. With only her pink spongy pads, Panda kneaded Amy's back. Amy said she enjoyed the cat massage more than the lotion licking.

My son-in-law often allowed Panda to sit on his shoulder while he reclined and watched TV. One evening after consuming Christmas cookies, he nodded off. Panda decided to tidy his beard. She stretched her neck over and nuzzled it up and down, in and out. I laughed as I watched her pay attention to detail while he slept.

Panda saved her best nurturing tactics for the dog. Maggie sprawled onto the living room rug without regard to anyone's movements around her. Panda snuggled alongside on the dog's pillow until she heard the time-to-groom snore alarm. She wasted no time gently washing the sides of Maggie's face and ears. Maggie's mouth formed a little smile. We didn't know whether she had dreams of doggie biscuits dancing in her head or if she enjoyed the special treatment—or both.

One day Amy took Panda to the vet for her checkup. I talked with her after she returned home.

"So, how did it go?"

"Everything went fine, but I didn't look forward to taking her," Amy said. "I knew it would require getting the cat into a carrier. Sometimes you can draw back a bleeding hand. It's not easy."

"I never had a cat carrier. I always swaddled my cats in bath towels."

"A carrier is better. At least you can drive without holding the cat."

"True. Did your husband have to help you?"

"He intended to help. He came into the kitchen trying to hide a chuckle. He said he couldn't wait to see how the cat responded to the carrier. We prepared ourselves for a challenge. I sat it down on the floor and opened the door. When I couldn't find Panda in the living room, I asked where she was. He started laughing and pointed to the carrier. I found her sitting inside. She looked up and gave me a ready-to-go wink."

"Panda's one amazing animal."

"That's not all. When I opened the carrier door at the vet's, she tiptoed out like her number had been called and sashayed back in when it was time to leave. Even the veterinarian said he'd never seen such behavior from a cat."

Panda enjoyed sleeping under the Christmas tree in her new home. But she never tried to climb it or disturb any of the decorations. When the day came for the home photo shoot, Odin wore his favorite yellow plaid shirt and smiled with delight. Panda posed beside him in front of the tree with elegant grace, welcoming his outstretched hand. Amy clicked the camera. Everyone received their Christmas card of Odin and Panda in time for the holidays.

I'm glad Amy turned down choosing one of the popular kittens. Having a cat like Panda helped us all experience lessons of love. Panda received the care she needed from her adopted family, and she repaid them with attention and affection they never expected.

22

The Queen and Her Castle

Edith Sickler

er eyes were pure peridot.

They were not the ordinary yellowish-green like most of her kind. They were stunning peridot. She was beautiful, and I told her that often, though I don't think she believed me.

Her coloring was unique too. She was mostly a soft, luxurious gray with splotches of yellow and white. I learned from some cat aficionados that she was a "muted tortie" or a tortoiseshell cat with a fur shading not too common in domestic shorthairs.

When I first saw her, she was following her momma outside, along with several siblings of various colors. Her mother was mostly white with some calico yellow features, and her hair was long. She seemed tame, as if she had lived with humans before being rejected and deposited in our neighborhood—pregnant and forced to find food. I called her Callie. Her mate was probably a handsome bum of unknown origin.

The kittens were born under a neighbor's storage building. The neighbor and I fed them and made sure they had water. One kitten was orange, and I named him Sunshine. Several were black and white, and the little gray one with colors I first called Gray Baby. I intended to socialize them and find them homes.

One day, the neighbor told me the development's owner told him to quit feeding the cats as he was going to trap and euthanize them. He didn't want feral cats hanging around the homes.

I quickly sought out the owner and told him I was trying to socialize the kittens and find homes for them. He said "God bless you" and that he would cease and desist temporarily.

The neighbor had stopped feeding Momma and her kittens, so I started enticing them to come to my porch to eat. I sat near their food dish, petting them as they ate and moving the food dish closer to the porch door. Gray Baby was the most hesitant to come in, but eventually she did, although she was very frightened and timid. She did not allow anyone to pick her up to hold her.

I took all the kittens to the veterinarian for a checkup and necessary medical procedures and found homes for all but two of them. Sunshine and Gray Baby remained in our home. They became our adopted fur babies to live with us and our black rescue cat, Midnight.

I wanted a better name for Gray Baby, similar to what we had been calling her. Finally, we decided the name Gracie fit her perfectly, and that became her name.

Gracie kept to herself most of the time. She came out to eat, and she faithfully used the litter box. She sometimes let us briefly pet her but then would quickly retreat. She would occasionally rub against my husband's leg and let him pet her. She seemed to trust him a little. She remained aloof all the years we had her, even though we were always sweet to her, trying to coax her out of her shell. She wasn't much trouble and was a beautiful recluse.

Sometimes Gracie would sit around with the other cats, but it wasn't often. Sometimes they tried to play with her, but she usually didn't respond to their efforts. One time, as she sat in the living room, Midnight walked past her, and Gracie gave her a big swat for no reason. It looked comical, and I couldn't help but ask her, "What was *that* about?" I guess it was because she thought she could.

The first Christmas we had with Gracie showed us another side of her personality. She watched from a safe vantage point as the decorations were placed around our home. She didn't bother anything. She never even batted at a low-hanging ball on the Christmas tree.

But on Christmas morning, everything changed. Gracie had a field day. The Angel of Christmas Present must have visited her during the night and anointed her queen. As presents were opened and papers, boxes, and ribbons dropped on the floor, she was the first of our felines to pounce right into the middle of the pile. All the cats then joined the fray and romped and played in the rattling papers and seemed to delight in the moment.

Suddenly, Gracie became Queen of the Christmas Papers. They were *hers*! She became aggressive . . . batting and hissing at the others and fussing with them until they gave up and left the area. She guarded the papers with her watchful eye for a good, long time, and finally fell asleep in the middle of them, tired out and contented, one paper draped over her. She had won. The papers were hers.

After placating her for a time, Sunny quietly crept up to the papers on the fringes of the stack so as not to awaken the Queen while gaining access to a corner of the Christmas paper. Nope. Gracie would have none of it. She chased him off in short order, maintaining her ownership. You know the stories of cats sleeping with one eye open.

This behavior was so unusual for her and so interesting to watch. It was a mini sideshow to the Christmas events that year in our home. The papers remained in place for several days before we felt we could clean them up. We left a few small papers for the cats to play in, and suddenly Gracie wasn't interested anymore. Her castle had been removed. And after experiencing the castle, she didn't care to fight over such a small prize.

The other cats happily tiptoed onto the remaining papers, curled up on them, and slept peacefully as Gracie retreated into her former life of an aloof, beautiful princess.

In all the years she was with us, Gracie never did become a friendly cat. And as for Christmas? She never bothered fighting over a pile of Christmas wrappings again.

She had had her moment, and she had claimed it.

23

Baby Jesus vs. Cats

Joanne O. McGaha

I grew up with a dog named Tillie from the time I was three months until I was sixteen. She was part dachshund, part visiting dog. Unfortunately, when I was in high school, the day came when she had to be put down. At school the next day, I told my girlfriends about it, and they cried with me.

That evening, a strange car appeared in our driveway. A boy from school whom I knew only slightly came to the door and handed me a tiny white kitten with muted color spots of gray and tan. He then gave me a litter box and food. "Here," he said, and he left with no further words.

At school the next day, I located the boy and told him we loved the kitten, but I didn't understand the gift. He said that he had overheard me telling my friends about Tillie and decided his mom didn't need that cat. After explaining my situation to her, she happily agreed.

We called the cat Rhoda, named after a character on the *Mary Tyler Moore Show.* Rhoda was Mary's friend on the show—an independent female who did her own thing and didn't care what others thought. My cat had those qualities.

When Rhoda was two years old, I adopted a little black kitten named Gus (as in Augustus because I got him in August). Rhoda immediately took on the role of mother and tried so very hard to train him in her ways. She would flatten him on his back and bathe him. It was so comical to watch him with his eyes shut tight as he submitted to her ministrations. Once, when they were outside on the patio, she went into the woods and brought back a mole, setting it in front of Gus. He merely watched as it scurried away. She retrieved it, again setting it before him, and again he did nothing. How frustrating.

Thus began my years as a cat fancier. I have had ten cats so far. All had such different personalities and physical and emotional characteristics. But what they had in common was that—like most cats—my cats climbed trees.

So it should not be a mystery why cats get excited when suddenly a tree appears in the main living room of the house in which they live. That tree is full of shiny, wiggly things that catch the light and seem to move at the slightest touch. When cats follow their natural instincts to investigate and to climb, often the tree falls down, the shiny objects break in the process, and humans get upset. Cats do not understand.

My husband and I bought and restored a two-story Victorian-era farmhouse, circa 1871. We furnished the house with antiques, except in the kitchen and family room. You can imagine the delight we took in decorating our home at Christmas.

Each year on Thanksgiving weekend, we went to a local tree farm, cut our own Christmas tree, and brought it home. We placed it in the family room in a large, heavy crock filled with water to keep it fresh. Our cats used the crock as a new source of water to drink. With three fully grown cats crawling underneath the tree, decorations on the lower branches had to be put back in place daily.

The house had a dining room we'd furnished with an antique table and chairs that seated twelve people. The antique buffet measured forty inches high and four feet in length. It had a mirror in the carved backdrop and was the perfect place on which to place the manger scene, complete with plastic figurines of Mary, head bent looking lovingly into the manger, her arms folded prayerfully across her chest; Joseph holding a lantern; shepherds, wise men, and of course, cows, sheep, and camels. The figurines were not tiny, except for Baby Jesus. He had been crafted draped in a blue blanket and was about two and a half inches in length. I cut straw in small pieces to tuck into the manger. The scene made a beautiful display on the buffet, especially with the mirror in the background, and I added tall candles at each end.

One morning when I passed by the buffet, I noticed Baby Jesus was missing from the manger. Puzzled, I glanced around the area but could not find him. None of the other figurines were gone, none were knocked over, and the straw was not disturbed. I went into the kitchen, and in the process of filling the cats' water dish, I discovered Baby Jesus floating in the dish. I fished him out, dried him off, and placed him back in the manger. Of course, the culprit was one of the cats, but which one?

At that time, we had three cats in residence. SAM—as in Southern Appalachian Migrant because we found him in

Kentucky—was a yellow, tail-less cat who was large even as a kitten. Strudel, who as a kitten had stepped into a bowl of strudel I was making when I turned to answer the phone; I found her happily devouring the batter. She loved sweets to the point of quivering if she was offered a donut. We tried to explain to her that she was a carnivore and was not supposed to eat sugar-laden carbohydrates, but she was addicted. Pokey, named Pocahontas though I'm not sure why, I captured from a stack of hay bales in a friend's barn when he said I could have any of the kittens I could catch. Fully grown, she had become an unassuming, gentle little lady.

Whichever cat the culprit was, he or she would have had to jump forty inches from the floor to the top of the buffet. I had read that cats have been known to jump seven times higher than they are tall. If SAM had jumped up there and taken the Baby Jesus, he would have destroyed the entire display. It was not in his demeanor to be dainty. Strudel? Only if the figurine was made of flour and sugar and smelled like donuts. That left Pokey. The manger scene was not visible to the cats from the floor so she must have sensed something was up there, and she would need to determine if it was in her realm of interest.

Pokey kidnapped Baby Jesus two more times, but not two days in a row. We never did see her perform her leap and jump back down carrying her treasure. But one morning when we were at the breakfast table, Pokey came trotting into the kitchen with Baby Jesus in her mouth and proudly deposited him into the water dish. She gazed at it for a few seconds then walked away, tail held high with the familiar crook at the very end.

I did not put Baby Jesus back in the manger. I put him on a higher shelf and tried to remember to put him back in the manger if we were having guests.

How does one know what goes on in the brain of a cat? What was Pokey trying to do? Or was she just playing with our minds? Each Christmas when I arrange the manger scene, I reminisce about the mysterious reason Pokey felt Baby Jesus belonged in water. And I smile.

24

How We Survived a Christmas Kitten

Jenny Lynn Keller

I have a theory about people and pets. Sometimes we choose them, but many times they choose us. Have I researched the subject extensively or conducted a thorough and peer-reviewed scientific study? Absolutely not. I simply base my notion on personal experience and an abundance of pets enriching my life.

My theory originated the second Christmas my husband and I were married. We'd purchased our first house several months earlier and were settled enough for an addition—a cat. Despite several well-meaning folks telling us Christmas wasn't the best time to add a pet to the family, my husband went to a friend's house to select a black kitten from a litter ready to find new homes. He returned with a gray tabby.

Was my husband color-blind? Were all the black kittens gone by the time he arrived?

Nope. He claimed the tabby ran out to meet him while all the black ones stayed close to their mother. His premise was that a friendly cat would make a better pet. But I had my heart set on a black one because they're usually feisty and playful. Oh, no need to worry about those personality traits, he declared. This tabby fit the description perfectly.

During the car ride home, the kitten wouldn't stay in its box, so my husband contained it inside his zipped-up jacket. The kitten had no alternative but to squeeze between his shirt buttons and onto his skin, where she crawled around trying to find an opening. Was she successful? Let's just say the answer depended on your perspective. As the kitten enjoyed seeing daylight once again and watched my husband tend to his scratched chest, we discussed the little girl's fate. Keep her or return to sender?

She stayed, and we named her Samantha, a big word for such a small fur ball. Our next major decision arrived at bedtime. Where would she sleep? In our waterbed with us wasn't an option because we already knew the damage her needle claws could do. The adjoining bathroom seemed the best choice, so I made her a fluffy bed with a blanket, tucked her inside it, flipped on the night light, and closed the door.

Early the next morning I woke up staring into cat eyes. Samantha lay on my pillow and purred like a small diesel engine. How did that happen when the bathroom door was still closed?

Since it was Saturday, the only day I could sleep late, I returned her to the bathroom and went back to bed. Hours later

I woke up to Samantha on my pillow and my husband sleeping through both cat encounters. How was the sneaky little feline escaping her room? I put her back on the blanket, secured the door shut, and waited to see what would happen.

Within minutes, two furry paws appeared under the door, latched onto the hardwood floor, and squeezed the rest of her body under the two-inch opening. The tiny stinker wanted to be with us and exploited one of our old house's novelties to achieve her goal.

This ranch house was among hundreds built in a little-known Tennessee location during World War II to house people working on a top-secret military project. Thousands of acres were cleared for the project, and lumber milled from the cut trees was used in construction of the buildings. As a result, these older houses had amenities people pay high dollars for today—solid oak floors, solid hickory kitchen cabinets, and lots of built-in wood storage shelves.

But in the years since our house's construction, subsequent owners installed carpet and sawed off the bottom of all doors to accommodate the height of the carpet on the floor. When we purchased the house, we removed the carpeting and refinished the gorgeous hardwood floors. Having an extra inch or so at the bottom of each door never fazed us—until Samantha joined our family.

The solution? We added a second mattress cover to the waterbed, hoped for the best, and now shared the space with a friendly kitten. But where would she stay while we were at work?

After a quick analysis of possibilities, we believed Samantha should stay in the basement. The structure's original occupant was allowed special features in the house, so there was a finished walkout basement leading to an in-ground pool. To our delight, the concrete basement walls were as thick as the sides of the pool. No way a feisty cat would escape this place when the staircase door was closed.

On Monday afternoon we returned home from work, descended to the basement, and found no kitten. By some crazy chance had she discovered a route upstairs? We checked everywhere and didn't find her. I was concerned she'd weaseled her way under the exterior door, so we checked the pool area. Thank goodness, nothing in the pool besides water.

But where was she?

A second and third hunt through the basement left us bewildered and speechless—and me almost in tears. Our Christmas kitten was gone.

Then we heard a muffled meow. But from where? We called her name and heard the sound again—from above. How did Samantha climb into the ceiling? The walls were painted concrete, and no furniture came close to touching the particleboard tiles covering the drop ceiling. They were two-feet square and heavy. How could a kitten move one of them?

We decided to rescue her first and figure out the mystery later. My husband fetched a ladder from the nearby utility room, pinpointed the approximate meow location, and removed a tile. Sure enough, our adventurous feline perched an arm's length away, her face dusty and body covered with cobwebs. After hugs from both of us, she received a necessary and unappreciated bath.

While Samantha air-dried and ate supper in the kitchen, we explored how she accomplished her amazing ceiling feat. A closer look at the bathroom window curtains gave us a clue. The determined pint-sized rascal must have climbed up them to the rod, stood on the rod to push her paws over the metal frame holding up the tiles, and pulled herself up and under a tile. Once on top of the drop ceiling, she walked across the entire basement to the far corner where we found her.

Did she think we were upstairs and want to be with us? Had she devised and executed a daytime version of her recently successful nighttime escape? If so, our freshly washed ball of fluff would make a superb cat burglar considering she could find a way out of anywhere she didn't want to be.

The next morning, we declared Samantha's new daycare center to be the entire main floor. We returned home after work to find her curled up on my bed pillow.

That Saturday we bought a live Christmas tree, set it up in the living room near the couch, covered every inch with keepsake decorations donated by our parents, and woke up in the middle of the night to a loud crash. Sure enough, the Christmas tree sprawled sideways across the couch like it was taking a nap.

Grateful none of the antique glass Christmas balls were broken, we righted the tree and wondered what had happened. How did a five-foot Douglas fir topple over when it was held and weighted down by a heavy cast-iron tree stand? A missing kitten should have been an obvious clue. A second clue should have been finding her wedged under the couch. But we were sleepy and went back to bed.

Finding the tree in the same reclining position when we returned from church the following afternoon left no doubt as to what was causing the problem. Samantha rested on a branch near the tree topper like she wanted the place of honor herself. What were we going to do with this curtain-climbing, tree-hopping kitten?

First, we removed the glass ornaments and stored them for safekeeping, hoping we could use them next year when our curious kitten would be a year older and might know the difference between a Christmas tree and a playground. Secondly, we placed a brick on each foot of the three-pronged tree stand. No way that tree was taking another nap on our couch.

Did our cat counterweights work? Yes, and we celebrated many Christmases with Samantha in the following years. Did the glass ornaments adorn the trees we decorated during those holiday seasons? I'm afraid not, since our Christmas kitten never lost her love of Christmas trees. She continued to climb every one we had.

But what's an old ornament compared to the love and affection of a pet wanting to be ours from the first moment she saw us? Wanting to be near us as much as possible. Wanting to sleep on my pillow every night of her life. Traveling high and low to find us so she could be near the family she chose to be hers.

Merry Christmas, everyone.

a Christmas cat haiku
snow and icicles
on cold December mornings
paws on frosted glass

25

Cat Toys for Christmas

Claudia Wolfe St. Clair

Before we get started, I have a couple of confessions to make. First, I don't have a cat. I never have. But all my children do, and so do my best friends. So I have grandcats, cat nieces, and cat nephews. And none of them live near me.

The second thing I have to confess is that I don't shop online. I'm guessing I might be one of a handful of people on earth who don't. For these two infractions, I hope you will forgive me.

However, these two infractions form the basis of what I want to share with you.

Our Covid winter dictated that we would not be travelling anywhere to be with anyone over the Christmas holidays.

That turned out to include *all* holidays over the course of an entire year.

Because I don't shop online, I started thinking about Christmas in early fall since I would be making everything. It takes a great deal of lead time to create gifts that go in the mail.

My son Colin called with a special request. His cat, Dusty, was particularly fond of balled-up socks. Not sweat socks, mind you. Dusty preferred expensive wool socks.

"Do you remember when you made all of those mice Christmas ornaments?" Colin said.

Did I remember? I've been making them since we lived in Panama a few dozen years ago. "Yes, I remember."

"Well, could you make a bigger version comparable to the size of a balled-up pair of socks? Dusty keeps stealing my socks. Oh yeah, and it needs to be made of wool."

Wool? That was pretty specific.

The first step was find the well-worn pattern. I'd moved into the house on Lake Erie a few years ago but hadn't finished unpacking. With every missing item, "it's in a box somewhere." By a stroke of good luck, I guessed the correct box right out of the gate. Pattern found! Next step, enlarge it.

As a retired art therapist, I have a huge assortment of art supplies and materials for upcycling at my disposal. I also knit. Somewhere in my stash of stuff were some lovely knitted items I'd created that I'd managed to shrink beyond redemption. I'd also been given a damaged, handknit Aran sweater that could not be salvaged. I'd saved it for years, waiting for just the right project. It was the perfect choice for a big mouse for Dusty.

One sleeve was sacrificed. I cut out the three pieces that would form the entire mouse body. Because it had not been shrunk, I chain-stitched around each piece to prevent fraying and to stabilize the shapes. It was an enjoyable endeavor assembling the big fat mouse. Mismatched buttons for eyes stitched through button to button would foil a cat from biting them off. Ears and tail were secured. I was very happy with the outcome.

My thoughts turned to the other friends and family with cats. Wouldn't it be good to tuck mouse cat toys into their packages?

Going back to the original pattern size, I started gathering materials for cat toys. There was a pair of socks I had made with some exquisite wool yarn. It was great to work with—extremely soft with simply wonderful colors. It was the first pair of socks I'd made with expensive sock yarn. It was also the first pair I'd managed to shrink into solid felt. But I could not bear to get rid of them.

Now I finally found the perfect use for those socks. Each one was enough to make three mice! They went together like a dream.

Tails and ears went on, but this time I opted to skip putting anything on for eyes. I figured the cat nieces for whom these were intended would blind these mice in no time. These would be three blind mice with tails intact. No farmer's wife in sight!

The cat toys were a big hit that Covid Christmas. Colin sent a video of Dusty batting his big fat mouse all over the hallway. Mission accomplished.

Just recently I was able to visit my cat nieces for the first time in over a year. They hadn't forgotten me. They checked me out as I settled into my favorite chair. They sniffed at my cup of tea, generally making me feel welcome. At my feet? Three blind mice, their cat toys from last Christmas.

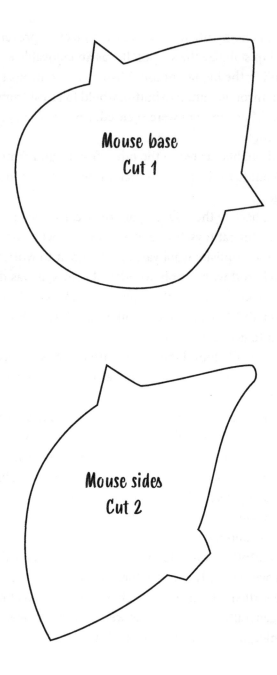

Mouse base
Cut 1

Mouse sides
Cut 2

Christmas Mouse Directions

Step 1: Cut 2 mouse body sides and 1 mouse base out of the fabric of your choice.

Step 2: With right sides together, match the square tabs on the two side pieces and pin edge.

Step 3: Hand stitch the seam about 1/4 inch from the edge to form the top of the mouse.

Step 4: Open out and pin the mouse sides to the base, right sides together, matching the pointed tabs and lining up the sewn seam with the center back and front of the base.

Step 5: Hand stitch (1/4-inch seam) around the base, leaving about 1/3 of the seam open on the end to enable stuffing.

Step 6: Turn the mouse right side out. Stuff with fiberfill or cotton wadding. Catnip or a bell can be added if you wish. Turn the raw edges under as you whipstitch the mouse body closed.

Step 7: Cut 2 circles out of thin leather or felt for the ears. Stitch to either side of the head. Cut a tail from the same material and stitch on where the back seam meets the base.

Step 8: Sew on small buttons or beads for eyes or use thread to embroider eyes.

26

Naughty and Nice

Lonnie Hull DuPont

I recently read a national cat-themed magazine that invited readers to send in the Christmas traditions they share with their cats. I considered contributing. But we haven't built Christmas traditions with our two cats. We've only built a list of things we can't do at Christmas because of our two cats.

This won't be a story about how my pet destroyed the Christmas tree. We never got that far.

Mary Kat and Tiki were littermates, same mother, different fathers. They were birthed one spring in Texas from a feral mother who was soon captured and taken away. Fortunately, two determined women found the vulnerable litter that had been left behind. One of those kind women, a friend of mine, took the kittens in. She had rescued and was caring for two nursing queens and their litters at the time, and once these kittens arrived at their new home, they lived a wonderful kittenhood. The nursing mothers took turns feeding the new babies alongside their own kittens, and a couple of feline uncles kept an eye on them all.

My husband, Joe, and I decided to adopt two females from the new litter. I flew down from Michigan to attend a conference in Texas and to pick up the kittens from my friend. Joe and I chose them based on their pictures. The black kitten we named Tiki. The silver tabby we named Mary Kat.

They were well-behaved little girls on the plane and in the car coming home. They were well-behaved in their special room after they moved in. They were super friendly. Mary Kat even high-fived our vet staff with her paw when she met them. We joked that they were so polite because they were from the South.

And the eye contact—I'd never had cats with such direct and open eye contact. They each lifted a paw as a question mark. Each slapped a tail once when her name was spoken. They were both chatty, probably because their mother was Siamese. Mary Kat vocalized in that Siamese way. Oh, the yowling . . . the drama . . . and that was when she was *happy* . . .

We confined the Texas newcomers to the laundry room at first. Then we opened the Pepto Bismol–pink bathroom next to the laundry room. Then the bedroom next to the bathroom. Eventually we gave them the run of the house.

And that's when we learned who they really were. I cover their velvety ears as I say this: What was I thinking, adopting two kittens at this point in my life?

By that, I mean that I was headed for hip replacement surgery very soon down the road. I was in a lot of pain when the

Texans arrived and was becoming less able to walk or lift things. Happily, successful surgery a couple years later would change that. But at the time we decided to adopt, I must have been crazy to get even one kitten, much less two kittens. When my cousin casually commented before I got them, "Two kittens in a house can be very destructive," I thought, *Nah, not mine.*

Alas. The problems started with surfaces. I know many cat people give their cats free run of dining tabletops, kitchen counters, and so forth. I never had. I'd never shared dinner with a cat on top of the table. I'd never let them roam the kitchen counters. With previous cats, I trained them to stay off the dining tables and kitchen counters and stove. I simply picked them up from where they should not be and put them on the floor and distracted them. This was done calmly. They were allowed to lounge atop one buffet near the dining table, and with the help of nubby fabrics and potted wheat grass, it was a spot they enjoyed. My previous cats were cool with that.

But with these two, by the time I could approach to pick them up from a forbidden surface, they'd already moved on. They were fast. And they did everything as a pair, so there were two of them to grab. In the first couple of years in their kittenhood, I could not train them at all. When they got bigger, for a couple of years I still was unable to lift and carry even one of them.

Hence, they became house cats who did what they pleased. Romping on the countertops. Sprawling on the dining table. Chasing each other over every high place they could find and destroying whatever was in their path.

Our nice kittens from Texas became naughty cats from Anywhere.

We had to kitten-proof the house in ways we hadn't antic-ipated. Joe duct-taped to keep kitties from going behind the washer and dryer. The girls loved to get behind the bedroom television and push on it; Joe secured that. I put away breakable tchotchkes that I had sitting around—including my vintage flamingos in the pink bathroom. The little Texans broke a large wing off one, and I caught on right away that this would keep happening.

I stopped leaving cabinet doors open because Tiki and Mary Kat hid together in the back where I couldn't reach them for as long as they deemed fun. I began to be sure to put away things that could spill—like the loosely capped bottle of vanilla kefir that they knocked to the floor. The kefir splattered the black refrigerator and wood cabinets like blood at a crime scene. I was still finding spots of it weeks later.

They loved diving into open drawers, so I had to stop leav-ing these open—a bad habit my entire life. If I left a drawer open just a smidge, they'd worm it open the rest of the way, dump the drawer on the floor somehow, and paw through to find fun things. I can't count how many times it looked like they were trotting around the house carrying prey in their mouths only to find it was one of my beaded bracelets.

They pulled down anything that could skid and fall. They took down table lamps, so I switched to using only floor lamps. But they still destroyed an antique floor lamp while I sat right next to it. I watched them merrily ride it down together until it smashed all over the floor. That time I cried.

One day, I lay down for a nap in the bedroom. I heard the girls getting into things in the rest of the house. I just couldn't deal with it that day, and I let them roll. I listened to them run, jump, crash, and careen. For four hours. When they were done, they hopped onto the bed together and plopped down, side by side, on the pillow next to me. I snapped a picture of them. In the photo, they look exhausted—but oh so satisfied.

I had gone through the 1989 San Francisco earthquake, and after such an event, you look at a room differently; you wonder what could fall on you. Now after living with Tiki and Mary Kat, I looked at a room differently yet again; I wondered what they could destroy. As our first Christmas together approached, I could see that my holiday world would have to change. Nothing was going to survive these two—starting with a Christmas tree. We didn't even bother. They would have stripped it in no time, just like they did any plant I brought into the house.

So what could we do to decorate for Christmas? I experimented in December a couple of years ago. One of the congregants in our church was a gardener who potted flora to sell. I bought a small cactus from him, perfectly shaped like a miniature Christmas tree, potted in a bright red pot. Adorable. Festive.

I took the cactus home and set it on the counter. Mary Kat went right for it. The cactus pricked her nose. She drew back and considered this. Then she leaned in and continued trying to get close to the green, pricking her nose over and over—until she found the *one* spot she could chew on without getting poked.

The cactus moved to Joe's workplace.

Next the bin of cardinals. That gorgeous songbird in my yard has extra meaning to me. But china and porcelain cardinals are breakable. I decided to try them anyway. I lined them up on the kitchen windowsill, which was not a place the girls usually noticed.

They noticed. But there was only mild interest—sniffing, then moving on. Whew. I could display breakable cardinals at Christmas.

Could we put out our nativity scene? Doubtful. The figures were freestanding, and knowing these two, the babe tucked into the manger would be fished out and batted around. Eventually Baby Jesus would be lost.

I donated the nativity scene to the church.

We stopped putting wrapped presents out—I bagged them and put them in the pantry. Plus I only wrapped them when the girls were having their daytime sleep.

I found an antique metal tree to hold Christmas cards. I thought it might be too tempting, but this they only studied for a moment. After rubbing cheeks on the cardboard edges of some cards, the cats moved on. Hooray! Displaying Christmas cards certainly helped with Christmas cheer.

Time marches on, of course, and as I write this, Tiki and Mary Kat are seven years old. I was informed that two years should be the end of kittenhood, but it wasn't for the Texans. For years, I had to keep my knitting in the car; I only knitted at other people's houses. That string of yarn and those moving, clicking needles were just too much temptation for the feline brain.

Now they've calmed down enough that I can knit in front of them if I'm careful. And that makes me think that this Christmas I should experiment again to find more Christmas items they might leave alone.

Here's the good news. At some point, I turned from feeling annoyed with Tiki and Mary Kat at Christmas to simply feeling happy to have them with us. They're aging, even though they don't yet show it. And I'm grateful for that. We have our pets for so short a time, and I treasure their energy now. If we arrange the house for them, that's okay—they have proven to be worth the trouble. They have proven to be the very best of companions.

Now instead of pining to decorate the house for Christmas, I think of how these sweet girls offer beauty to our home every day of the year. When Joe comes home from work and needs a quick nap, nobody's happier than the Texans. Anywhere, anytime, they will snuggle alongside him. When I'm not feeling up to snuff, they tuck in on either side of me, watching me. They are wonderful nurses.

When Mary Kat is such a still-kittenish handful at Christmas that I laugh out loud, I'm reminded of the joy of new birth. When I'm stressed by the holidays and Tiki crawls up onto my chest, looks right into my eyes, and touches my chin with her paw, I know I have been given the most remarkable gift—deep understanding from one of the Creator's most complex creatures.

Tiki and Mary Kat were welcome gifts in our house from the get-go. But who knew those gifts would age so nicely and get better and better at living with us—enough so that every day with them feels festive.

Joe and I couldn't ask for more.

27

Every Day Is Boxing Day When You Live with Cats

Susan C. Willett

In England and many of the former British colonies, December 26 is Boxing Day—a day in which people watch sports, shop huge sales, and visit with friends and family. It's a little like Black Friday in the US, an extra holiday tacked on to the main event, only in this case at Christmas instead of Thanksgiving.

Historians and experts debate the reason it's called Boxing Day, though they agree it has nothing to do with breaking down cardboard for recycling or putting unwanted items back into their original packages for regifting—or people punching each other.

Some say Boxing Day has its roots in traditional acts of charity toward workers and the less fortunate: the wealthy giving their servants gifts after they worked on Christmas or bringing boxes of food to the poor.

My husband and I—and our three dogs and four cats—don't live in England. But we celebrate our own version of Boxing Day because we are citizens of a former British colony, because the feline citizens of our home demand it, and because we always seem to have boxes to spare.

In this age of online ordering, boxes land on our front porch at least once a week. But during the holidays, our BPD (Boxes Per Day) can increase dramatically as we order presents for family, friends, colleagues, and pets—and sometimes find ourselves on the receiving end of such gifting. For our cats, therefore, the joys of the season mean the joys of boxes.

The first step when a parcel is brought into our home is the ritual Inspection of the Boxes. Thorough sniffage of all accessible sides of each box is required. Once the felines of the house have cleared them, it is time for Unboxing. On the internet, Unboxing is a thing: people recording themselves on video opening packages and describing what's inside. But in a house with cats, that would be a bit of a challenge, because what's inside—as soon as physically possible—is a cat.

Even if there is a gift for said cat in the box, the box is its own gift—one to be explored and savored. Experts have long debated what draws cats to boxes, but there are no definitive explanations, and the cats aren't talking. And there are oh so many ways to enjoy a box.

For one thing, they are good for sitting in. Or lying upon. I have been known to celebrate Boxing Day by constructing a box castle, taping a whole bunch together in a multistory cardboard creation with several layers, multiple hidey holes, and long tunnels that beg investigation from curious cats. I have also tempted our kitties by putting a box inside a box. Our tuxedo cat Calvin particularly enjoyed that one, sitting inside the double box with an expression that combined contentment with a touch of gloat and giving new meaning to the concept of a boxed set.

Calvin's sister, Elsa Clair, is also a box aficionado, but her eyes glow with delight when a box comes with packing paper—an added bonus that takes jumping into the cardboard to a whole new level of noisy enjoyment. One of Elsa Clair's favorite games is Pounce the Toy in the Packing Paper. But the most fun in the world for that cat is when I take the paper out of the box and lay it on our living room floor so she can take a running leap after a tossed fuzzy pink mouse and skid across the paper in a flurry of crinkle and claws—kind of like an indoor wintertime version of a Slip 'N Slide, but without the water.

Years ago, an item we ordered came with corrugated packaging that formed the outline of a rectangle; there was no top or bottom, just a several-inches-tall cardboard wall. Athena, our dilute tortie, thought this Not-a-Box was the bomb. She sat within its borders, pleased as Christmas punch. Athena will sit on—or in—anything vaguely boxlike. Or, to be honest, she'll sit on anything that is on any thing. I think it's a cat thing. Either way, we have continued the Not-a-Box tradition ever since the first one, fashioning our own Not-a-Boxes for Athena's pleasure. What we do for our cats . . .

Dawn—Athena's torbie sister—likes her boxes upside down and propped open by the flaps. A box set up this way is perfect for hide-and-sneak. Or a game of ankle hunting. For years, we left a particularly beloved box in our second-floor hallway near the top of the steps, because it was Dawn's favorite place to hang out. Coming up the stairs, I'd see two large eyes peering from within the darkness under the propped box. Sometimes I could hear the swishy sound of a tail flick against the cardboard walls. I learned to walk by with just enough distance between me and the box o' cat—approximately the length of an outstretched paw.

One year, I accidently left a particularly large empty box sitting by the front door, its flaps not quite closed. Elsa Clair surveyed the situation and blithely hopped in, letting the flaps close over her and hide her completely.

She was silent. There was no movement from within that cardboard enclosure. And I knew—just knew—that cat was plotting something.

I grabbed my iPhone, set the photo app to Video, and clicked on the red Record button, waiting for chaos to ensue. I was sure this was going to be the best video. It would go viral. I'd get a million likes. My cat and I would be internet famous.

As I sat on the cold hallway floor, I envisioned forty-seven different scenarios, each generating more LOLs than the last.

Elsa Clair would contain her coiled energy only so long before she burst out of the box like the creature in the movie *Alien*.

Or maybe Calvin would hop on the box, unaware of the danger that lurked beneath the cardboard, until an Elsa Clair earthquake rocked the surface, tumbling the man cat off as he scrambled for safety.

Or perhaps my dog Tucker would drop his ball on the box and paw it several times before the flaps seemed to move of their own accord, causing the poor dog to abandon his

Precious until he figured out what devilment was toying with his terrier brain.

It could be anything, but I was sure it was going to be spectacularly funny.

In less than a minute, Calvin approached the box. This was it! I braced myself as he stretched himself out, low to the floor, his sniffs audible as he assessed the situation.

And . . . nothing. Elsa Clair stayed silent. There wasn't a hint of movement from her boxy lair.

A sudden jangly sound of a dog floppity startled Calvin, and he walked away.

That sound was Jasper, who sauntered into the hall. He's got a good hound-y nose, I thought; maybe he would investigate the primed and loaded box.

And . . . nothing. Not a creature was stirring inside that box. I began to doubt myself; maybe Elsa Clair had hopped out when I wasn't looking? But I was looking; I was recording the whole time. How could she have left without me noticing? Or maybe she had become a new twist on Schrödinger's cat—simultaneously existing and not existing within the box.

Jasper walked in front of my camera, without a glance in the box's general direction. He had no idea Elsa Clair was in there.

Then my very intelligent border collie, Lilah, strolled in. I could tell she knew something was in the box. Inhaling deeply, she thoroughly inspected the package. From two different angles. Slowly. Deliberately. Carefully.

I was sure Elsa Clair would pop out and surprise Lilah and I'd have recorded it and then I'd post it on YouTube where it would get a bazillion jillion views (a number I had learned the previous weekend from a young friend I met at a holiday party).

And . . . nothing.

By then Lilah had figured out there was a cat in the box, which was no big deal since this was obviously not an unusual occurrence in our home. She left to find a comfy spot to curl up in and take a nap.

I was about to give up and stop recording when I observed a slight twitch to one of the box flaps. Now, I thought, Elsa Clair will make a grand and glorious, fast and furious, can't-contain-curious leap from her hiding spot. I was ready. I thought at least I'd capture that: my cat springing up like a jack-in-the-box.

And . . . our normally light-speed cat oozed slowly out of the box. She took a moment to contemplate the ceiling. Briefly reconsidered whether to rebox herself. Flicked her tail. And with an adagio grace, exited stage left.

In the end, I wound up with two minutes of video illustrating exactly what life with dogs and cats is like. It's full of surprises, but not the ones you expect.

And while I did post the resulting video on my blog and Facebook page, I never got my bazillion jillion views.

Nowadays you can buy boxes designed for cats. Target sells holiday-themed cardboard constructions, complete with internal scratchers. But me? I'm more of a do-it-yourselfer and a traditionalist. I like a good old-fashioned plain box. And I love to watch the look on Elsa Clair's furry little face, when—on Boxing Day or any other day—we open a package and there's packing paper inside. It's like Christmas morning for Elsa Clair. And that joy is wonderfully contagious.

Which is why I will admit I bought a roll of packing paper for my cat.

And it came in a box.

ABOUT the CONTRIBUTORS

Anita Aurit is an award-winning writer and blogger who lives with three cats in North Idaho and believes everything is more interesting from a feline point of view. She has received multiple awards for her blog, *Feline Opines*, and she received a Certificate of Excellence from the Cat Writers' Association for her book, *Are There Head Bonks in Heaven?* You can find Anita at felineopines.net/ and anitaaurit.wixsite.com/anitaaurit.

Suzanne Baginskie has sold many short mysteries and romance stories, and twenty-one of her nonfiction stories have been published in *Chicken Soup for the Soul* books. The recently released romantic suspense novel *Dangerous Charade* is the first book in her FBI Affairs series. Suzanne is a member of Mystery Writers of America, Florida Mystery Writers of America, Sisters-in-Crime, and the Short Mystery Fiction Society.

Lisa Begin-Kruysman is the author of several animal-inspired books. Her work has garnered multiple honors from national writing competitions including those sponsored by the Dog Writers Association of America. Originally from Hackensack, New Jersey, and later the New Jersey Shore region, she now writes from the small coastal town of St. Marys, Georgia.

Claudia Fanti Brooks is a licensed barber specializing in family hair styling. She lives with her husband, Dave, in Ohio, where they enjoy biking, hiking, boating, cooking together . . . and, of course, eating! They look forward to celebrating yet another Christmas with their two funny and handsome boy cats.

Deborah Camp is a freelance writer and three-time winner of sponsored awards from the Cat Writers' Association. Her stories, essays, articles, and op-eds have appeared in *Simply Pets*, *Lamplighter*, the *Phoenix Sun-Times*, *Writers Weekly*, the *Commercial Appeal*, and *Second-Chance Cats*. She is a monthly pet columnist for *The Best Times* and editor-in-chief for *Insights Magazine*. Camp is a happily retired small business owner and part-time adjunct professor of anthropology.

Debbie De Louise is a librarian at a public library and the author of twelve books, including several standalone mysteries and a cozy mystery series that features a library cat. Debbie's short stories and poetry have appeared in anthologies, and her cat-themed articles have been published in pet publications. A member of the Cat Writers' Association, Sisters-in-Crime, International Thriller Writers, and the Long Island Authors Group, Debbie lives on Long Island with her family and three cats. You can connect with her through her website debbie delouise.com.

Andrea Doering is an editor and the author of several children's books and short stories. She has been the lucky caretaker of six dogs thus far. She holds an MA in English/creative writing from the University of Maine and lives with her family in New York.

Rhonda Dragomir is a multimedia creative who treasures her fairy-tale life in Central Kentucky, insisting her home is her castle, even if her prince refuses to dig a moat. She has published works in several anthologies and periodicals and is seeking publication of her first novel, a sixteenth-century historical romance. She has won multiple awards, including being named 2019 Writer of the Year by Serious Writer, Inc. Read more about her on her website, www.rhondadragomir.com.

Lonnie Hull DuPont is an award-winning poet, editor, and author of several nonfiction books. Her poetry can be read in dozens of periodicals and literary journals, and her work has been nominated for a Pushcart Prize. She is a member of Cat Writers' Association and Dog Writers Association of America, and her nonfiction is frequently about animals, including her memoir, *Kit Kat and Lucy: The Country Cats Who Changed a City Girl's World*. She lives in southern Michigan with her husband and two highly evolved cats.

Karen Foster is a keynote speaker who writes articles and devotions that depict God's power in everyday lives. She is the author of *Lunch with Loretta: Discover the Power of a Mentoring*

Friendship, a nonfiction narrative book that shows two women in a multigenerational relationship who seek God. Karen is also a contributor to *The Horse of My Dreams: True Stories of the Horses We Love* and *Chicken Soup for the Soul: Military Families.* You can follow her at KarenFosterAuthor.com.

Sherri Gallagher (www.sherrigallagher.com) has been participating in K9 search and rescue since 1998. Her bestselling books (all available on Amazon) are based on her own dogs or SAR team member canines. Sherri's teen trilogy, Growing Up SAR, includes the novels *Turn, Go Find,* and *Bark Alert,* and her romance novels, *Sophie's Search, Out of the Storm, Pine Cone Motel,* and *Labrador Tea,* are part of her series Searching the North Country. Her Facebook page is SherriGallagherAuthor and the SAR team Facebook page is GSSARDA Illinois.

Jenny Lynn Keller is a gal raised in the South who loves her Appalachian Mountain heritage and transforms her family's rowdy adventures into stories filled with hope, humor, love, and plenty of Southern charm. As a contributor to *Daily Guideposts* and frequent speaker about the history, culture, and beauty of the Great Smoky Mountains and surrounding area, she highlights Southern Appalachian folklore and places of interest through her weekly blog at www.JennyLynnKeller.com. Her true horse story, "A Pinto for Pennies," appears in Callie Smith Grant's *The Horse of My Dreams.*

Sherry Diane Kitts writes nonfiction short stories. Her stories have been published in several anthologies: *Blessings in Disguise, Remembering Christmas,* and *Pandemic Moments.*

Sherry belongs to a Florida chapter of Word Weavers International. She hopes her writings are relatable, inspiring, and helpful to others through their life's journeys.

Linda L. Kruschke writes candid memoir and fearless poetry. She blogs at AnotherFearlessYear.net and AnchoredVoices.com and has been published in *Fathom Magazine, The Christian Journal, Bible Advocate, Now What?* online magazine, *ibelieve.com, Calla Press, Divine Purpose* blog and magazine, *Agape Review*, and several anthologies. She is editor of *Swallow's Nest*, the poetry journal of Oregon Christian Writers.

Andi Lehman freelances in diverse markets and writes nonfiction stories, articles, devotions, and grants. An author, editor, and popular speaker (live and virtual), she enjoys working with children and has just recently published *Saving Schmiddy*, her first book in a conservation series for kids. Her education company, Life with Animals, teaches the wonder of all creatures and our responsibility to care for them. To learn more about Andi's work with words and animals, visit AndiLehman.com.

Maggie Marton writes about dogs, cats, and kids—and often the intersection of all three—for print and web publications and on her award-winning blog, OhMyDogBlog.com. Maggie coauthored *Pet Blogging for Love and Money*, a guide to launching and running a profitable pet blog. She lives in the Indianapolis area with a dog, two cats, a tank of fish, two preschoolers, and a patient husband.

Joanne O. McGaha left high school following her junior year to enter Ohio State University as an early admissions student.

Three years later she had earned her degree in business administration, after which she worked in various financial management positions before retiring in 2020. She lives in northeast Ohio on the shores of Lake Erie with her husband, William McGaha.

Kim Peterson, owned throughout the years by five adventurous felines, knows life with a cat is filled with surprises. A freelance writer, editor, and conference speaker, Kim also mentors aspiring writers online for Taylor University. Her writing has appeared in various anthologies, including *Chicken Soup for the Caregiver's Soul*, *Rocking Chair Reader: Family Gatherings*, and *Moments with Billy Graham*. Meet Kim at naturewalkwith god.wordpress.com/welcome and encounter God's creation through her blog.

For close to twenty years, **Patricia Avery Pursley** was a freelance media relations agent representing Christian authors to national print and electronic media for interviews. Her creativity extended from the Santa Fe Natives sweater brand and designs to the Cowtown Cookie Company brand, product, and packaging, still on the market today. Currently living in the Houston area, she serves on the marketing committee for the Woodlands Arts Council. Patricia writes, gets creative in the kitchen, and might be found wandering distant shores with her husband, Tom.

Amy Shojai (www.SHOJAI.com) is a nationally known pet care expert and a certified animal behavior consultant for cats and dogs. She is the award-winning author of over thirty-five pet care books and a pet-centric thriller series featuring a trained Maine Coon cat and a German shepherd service dog. She lives in North Texas with Karma-Kat and Shadow-Pup, and the loving legacy of several furry muses, including Seren.

Edith (Eadie) Sickler, a second generation Finnish American who lived most of her life in Northeast Ohio and now lives in Florida, has a journalism background and is a freelance writer for a Florida newspaper. While staying home during the Covid pandemic, she wrote *Finland to America: One Family's Journey of Courage and Hope,* a book that highlights her grandparents' immigration from Finland, their lives in America, and the lives of their thirteen children. Published by Liberty Hill Publishing, the book includes Finnish recipes and photographs throughout and is sold online.

Lauraine Snelling is the award-winning author of over one hundred novels, including the beloved Red River of the North series. When not writing or gardening, she can be found, paintbrush in hand, creating flowers and landscapes. She and her husband, Wayne, live in the Tehachapi Mountains in California with their basset, Annie, a tortoiseshell cat named Lapcat who does her best to keep them rodent free, and five hens who lay eggs and dispose of mice who dare enter their yard.

Claudia Wolfe St. Clair is an artist, writer, art therapist, and *anamcara* from Toledo, Ohio. She is the mother of three and grandmother of six. She and the love of her life have restored the family home and gardens on Lake Erie. You can read more from Claudia in the Callie Smith Grant collections *The Horse of My Dreams, The Horse of My Heart, Second-Chance Dogs, Second-Chance Cats,* and *The Dog Who Came to Christmas.*

Nanette Thorsen-Snipes, a freelance writer and editor, has contributed stories or devotions to more than sixty-five compilation books, including *Personal Titanic Moments, Sweet Tea for the Soul, Guideposts* Miracle series, and *Chicken Soup for the Soul*, among others. She and her husband, Jim, have four children and eight grandchildren, plus two amusingly strange cats—Eli and Missy. You can find Nanette at www.faithworks editorial.com.

Susan C. Willett is a writer, humorist, and blogger whose award-winning original stories, poems, and humor appear in print and online, including her website LifeWithDogsAnd Cats.com and on Facebook, Twitter (@WithDogsAndCats), and Instagram (@lifewithdogsandcats). You can read more of her work in Callie Smith Grant's books *Second-Chance Dogs, Second-Chance Cats,* and *The Dog Who Came to Christmas* as well as in multiple Chicken Soup for the Soul books, including *The Magic of Cats, Listen to Your Dreams,* and *My Clever, Curious, Caring Cat.* She shares her home with dogs Lilah, Jasper, and Halley as well as cats Dawn, Athena, Elsa Clair, and Calvin T. Katz, The Most Interesting Cat in the World™, whose photo went viral and who now has his own social media accounts. Susan has plenty of inspiration for her work, often finding it hiding in a box, splashing through a mud puddle, or taking up an entire couch.

ABOUT the COMPILER

Callie Smith Grant enjoys animals of all kinds. She is the author of many published animal stories and several biographies, and she is the editor of the anthologies *The Dog Who Came to Christmas, Second-Chance Cats* (awarded the Muse Medallion from Cat Writers' Association), *Second-Chance Dogs* (awarded the Maxwell Medallion from Dog Writers Association of America), *The Horse of My Dreams, The Horse of My Heart, The Dog Next Door, The Cat in the Window, The Dog at My Feet,* and *The Cat in My Lap.*

ACKNOWLEDGMENTS

Many thanks to the talented writers in this book who have trusted us with their good work. Thanks to the decision-makers at Revell for wanting to publish a book of Christmas cat stories. And a special thanks to my ever-patient editor and brilliant friend, Dr. Vicki Crumpton, for extending wisdom and grace as always.